KW-361-779

CONDÉ NAST JOHANSENS

20 **J** 03

· RECOMMENDED ·

This pocket guide is designed to complement Condé Nast Johansens illustrated Guides by providing an instant reference to all 1,245 inspected and recommended Hotels, Country Houses, Inns and Resorts throughout Great Britain, Europe and North America.

The principal amenities available at each recommendation are represented by symbols, the definition of which can be found on pages 4–5.

The entries appear in alphabetical order; first by country and then by county, region, state or province.

Comprehensive illustrated information relating to each recommendation is available in our published A4 Guides or on our website.

Please remember to mention Condé Nast Johansens when you make a reservation and again when you check in. You will be made to feel very welcome.

www.johansens.com

CONTENTS

Recommended Hotels,
Country Houses, Small Hotels & Inns
Great Britain & Ireland

Recommmended Hotels
Europe & The Mediterranean

KEY TO SYMBOLS

ISDN/Modem point in all bedrooms

At least one non-smoking bedroom

Lift available for guests' use

Jacuzzi / whirlpool

Air conditioning in all bedrooms

Indoor swimming pool

Outdoor swimming pool

SPA A dedicated spa – offering extensive health, beauty & fitness treatments together with comprehensive water treatments

Tennis court at hotel

Croquet lawn at hotel

Fishing can be arranged

Golf course on site

Golf course nearby, which has an arrangement with the hotel allowing guests to play

Shooting can be arranged

Riding can be arranged

Skiing

Hotel has a helicopter landing pad

Licensed for wedding ceremonies

CONDÉ NAST JOHANSENS GUIDES

All the recommendations in this Pocket Guide can be found in
our range of published guides. The guides contain further
information about each property including large colour pictures,
descriptive text, directions, price details and location maps.

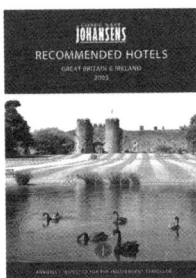

RECOMMENDED HOTELS,
GREAT BRITAIN & IRELAND

*440 unique and luxurious hotels, town houses, castles and
manor houses chosen for their superior standards and
individual character*

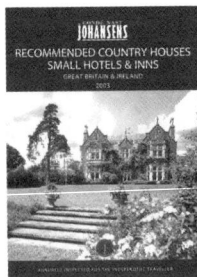

RECOMMENDED COUNTRY HOUSES,
SMALL HOTELS & INNS,
GREAT BRITAIN & IRELAND

*282 smaller more rural properties,
ideal for short breaks or more intimate stays*

CONDÉ NAST JOHANSENS GUIDES

To order these guides please call
From the UK: FREEPHONE 0800 269 397
From Europe: +44 208 655 7810
From the US: TOLL FREE 1-800-564-7518

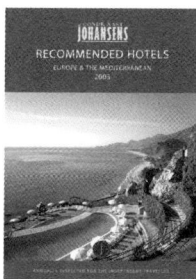

RECOMMENDED HOTELS,
EUROPE & THE MEDITERRANEAN

*324 continental gems featuring châteaux,
resorts and charming countryside hotels*

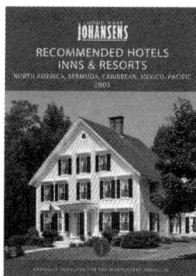

RECOMMENDED HOTELS, INNS & RESORTS,
NORTH AMERICA, BERMUDA, CARIBBEAN,
MEXICO, PACIFIC

*199 properties including many hidden
delights from across the region*

Airlines

Air France	www.airfrance.com
Alitalia	www.alitalia.com
American Airlines	www.aa.com
British Airways	www.britishairways.com
Cathay Pacific	www.cathaypacific.com
Continental Airlines	www.continental.com
Crossair	www.crossair.com
Delta Airlines	www.delta.com
easyjet	www.easyjet.com
Go Fly	www.go-fly.com
Iberia	www.iberia.com
KLM	www.klm.com
Lufthansa	www.lufthansa.com
Qantas	www.qantas.com.au
Ryanair	www.ryanair.com
Sabena	www.sabena.com
Scandinavian Airlines	www.scandinavian.net
Singapore Airlines	www.singapore-airlines.com
South African Airways	www.saa.co.za
United Airlines	www.unitedairlines.com
Virgin Atlantic	www.virgin-atlantic.com

Car Rentals

AVIS	www.avis.com
Budget rent-a-car	www.budget.com
Europcar	www.europcar.com
Hertz	www.hertz.com
Sixt	www.e-sixt.com

CONDÉ NAST
JOHANSENS

Condé Nast Johansens Ltd
6-8 Old Bond Street, London, W1S 4PH
Tel: +44 20 7499 9080 Fax: +44 20 7152 3565
E-Mail: info@johansens.com

Find Condé Nast Johansens on the Internet at:

www.johansens.com

Publishing Director – Great Britain & Ireland:	Stuart Johnson
Publishing Director – Europe:	Charlotte Evans
Publisher – North America:	Lesley O'Malley-Keyes
Production Manager:	Kevin Bradbrook
Production Controller:	Laura Kerry
Senior Designer:	Michael Tompsett
Sales & Marketing Director:	Tim Sinclair
Client Services Director:	Fiona Patrick
PA to Publishing Director:	Fiona Galley
Publishing Executive - Europe:	Claire Gorman
PA to Managing Director:	Siobhan Smith
Managing Director:	Andrew Warren

Whilst every care has been taken in the compilation of this Guide, the Publishers cannot accept responsibility for any inaccuracies or for changes since going to press, or for consequential loss arising from such changes or other inaccuracies, or for any other loss direct or consequential arising in connection with information relating to establishments listed in this publication.

No part of this publication may be copied or reproduced, stored in a retrieval system or transmitted, in any form or by any means, electronic, mechanical, photocopy, recording or otherwise, without the prior permission of the Publishers.

Copyright © 2002 Condé Nast Johansens Limited

2002 AWARDS FOR EXCELLENCE

The Condé Nast Johansens 2002 Awards for Excellence were
presented at the Awards Dinner held at The Dorchester
hotel, London on November 12th, 2001.

Awards were made to those properties worldwide that
represented the finest standards and best value for money
in luxury independent travel.

An important source of information for these awards was
the feedback provided by guests who completed Johansens
Guest Survey reports.

Most Excellent Country Hotel Award

Northcote Manor Country Hotel – Devon, England. p36

Most Excellent City Hotel Award

Hotel On The Park – Gloucestershire, England. p46

Most Excellent London Hotel Award

The Colonnade, The Little Venice Town House
– London, England. p65

Most Excellent Value for Money Award

The Gibbon Bridge Hotel – Lancashire, England. p58

Most Excellent Service Award

Combe House Hotel – Devon, England. p37

Most Excellent Restaurant Award

Maison Talbooth – Essex, England. p45

Most Excellent Coastal Hotel Award

The Grand Hotel – Eastbourne, England. p90

2002 AWARDS FOR EXCELLENCE

Most Excellent Country House Award
Glenapp Castle – Ballantrae, Scotland. p124

Most Excellent Traditional Inn Award
The Crown Hotel – Lincolnshire, England. p61

Europe: The Most Excellent City Hotel
Hotel Rector – Salamanca, Spain. p179

Europe: The Most Excellent Country Hotel
Château de Vault de Lugny– Avallon, France. p141

Europe: The Most Excellent Waterside Resort
Domaine de Rochevilaine – Billiers, France. p140

North America: Most Outstanding Hotel
Wheatleigh – Massachusetts, USA. p198

North America: Most Outstanding Inn
The Willows – California, USA. p189

North America: Most Outstanding Resort
Turtle Island –Yasawa Islands, Fiji p.220

Condé Nast Johansens Special Award for Excellence
Henderson Village – Georgia, USA. p192

Knight Frank Award for Excellence and Innovation
Nicholas Dickenson & Nigel Chapman

GREAT BRITAIN & IRELAND

England

COMBE GROVE MANOR HOTEL & COUNTRY CLUB

Brassknocker Hill, Monkton Combe, Bath, Somerset BA2 7HS

Tel: 01225 834644 **Fax:** 01225 834961

e-mail: reservations@combegrovemanor.com

THE BATH PRIORY HOTEL AND RESTAURANT

Weston Road, Bath, Somerset BA1 2XT

Tel: 01225 331922 **Fax:** 01225 448276

e-mail: bathprioryhotel@compuserve.com

THE BATH SPA HOTEL

Sydney Road, Bath, Somerset BA2 6JF

Tel: 0870 400 8222 **Fax:** 01225 444006

e-mail: fivestar@bathspa.u-net.com

THE QUEENSBERRY

Russel Street, Bath, Somerset BA1 2QF

Tel: 01225 447928 **Fax:** 01225 446065

e-mail: enquiries@bathqueensberry.com

The Royal Crescent Hotel

16 Royal Crescent, Bath, Somerset BA1 2LS

Tel: 01225 823333 **Fax:** 01225 339401

e-mail: reservations@royalcrescent.co.uk

The Windsor Hotel

69 Great Pulteney Street, Bath BA2 4DL

Tel: 01225 422100 **Fax:** 01225 422550

e-mail: sales@bathwindsorhotel.com

Apsley House

141 Newbridge Hill, Bath, Somerset BA1 3PT

Tel: 01225 336966 **Fax:** 01225 425462

e-mail: info@apsley-house.co.uk

Oldfields

102 Wells Road, Bath, Somerset BA2 3AL

Tel: 01225 317984 **Fax:** 01225 444471

e-mail: info@oldfields.co.uk

The County Hotel

18/19 Pulteney Road, Bath, Somerset BA2 4EZ

Tel: 01225 425003 **Fax:** 01225 466493

e-mail: reservations@county-hotel.co.uk

Villa Magdala

Henrietta Road, Bath, Somerset BA2 6LX

Tel: 01225 466329 **Fax:** 01225 483207

e-mail: jsvilla@villamagdala.co.uk

TASBURGH HOUSE HOTEL

Warminster Road, Bath BA2 6SH

Tel: 01225 425096

e-mail: hotel@bathtasburgh.co.uk

HOMEWOOD PARK

Hinton Charterhouse, Bath, Somerset BA2 7TB

Tel: 01225 723731 **Fax:** 01225 723820

e-mail: res@homewoodpark.com

HUNSTRETE HOUSE

Hunstrete, Nr Bath, Somerset BS39 4NS

Tel: 01761 490490 **Fax:** 01761 490732

e-mail: reservations@hunstretehouse.co.uk

BATH LODGE HOTEL

Norton St Philip, Bath, Somerset BA2 7NH

Tel: 01225 723040 **Fax:** 01225 723737

e-mail: info@bathlodge.com

THE CARPENTERS ARMS

Stanton Wick, Nr Pensford, Somerset BS39 4BX

Tel: 01761 490202 **Fax:** 01761 490763

e-mail: carpenters@dial.pipex.com

MOORE PLACE HOTEL

The Square, Aspley Guise, Milton Keynes, Bedfordshire MK17 8DW

Tel: 01908 282000 **Fax:** 01908 281888

e-mail: manager@mooreplace.com

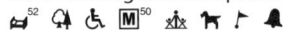

FLITWICK MANOR

Church Road, Flitwick, Bedfordshire MK45 1AE

Tel: 01525 712242 **Fax:** 01525 718753

e-mail: flitwick@menzies–hotels.co.uk

THE BERYSTEDE

Bagshot Road, Sunninghill, Ascot, Berkshire SL5 9JH

Tel: 0870 400 8111 **Fax:** 01344 872301

e-mail: berystede@macdonald-hotels.co.uk

MONKEY ISLAND HOTEL

Bray-on-thames, Maidenhead, Berkshire SL6 2EE

Tel: 01628 623400 **Fax:** 01628 784732

e-mail: monkeyisland@btconnect.com

THE LEATHERNE BOTTEL RIVERSIDE INN & RESTAURANT

The Bridleway, Goring-on-thames, Berkshire RG8 0HS

Tel: 01491 872667 **Fax:** 01491 875308

e-mail: leathernebottel@aol.com

FREDRICK'S HOTEL & RESTAURANT

Shoppenhangers Road, Maidenhead, Berkshire SL6 2PZ

Tel: 01628 581000 **Fax:** 01628 771054

e-mail: reservations@fredricks–hotel.co.uk

THE INN ON THE GREEN

The Old Cricket Common, Cookham Dean, Berkshire SL6 9NZ

Tel: 01628 482638 **Fax:** 01628 487474

e-mail: reception@theinnonthegreen.com

CLIVEDEN

Taplow, Berkshire SL6 0JF

Tel: 01628 668561 **Fax:** 01628 661837

e-mail: Reservations@clivedenhouse.co.uk

DONNINGTON VALLEY HOTEL & GOLF CLUB

Old Oxford Road, Donnington, Newbury, Berkshire RG14 3AG

Tel: 01635 551199 **Fax:** 01635 551123

e-mail: general@donningtonvalley.co.uk

THE VINEYARD AT STOCKCROSS

Newbury, Berkshire RG20 8JU

Tel: 01635 528770 **Fax:** 01635 528398

e-mail: general@the-vineyard.co.uk

THE REGENCY PARK HOTEL

Bowling Green Road, Thatcham, Berkshire RG18 3RP

Tel: 01635 871555 **Fax:** 01635 871571

e-mail: info@regencyparkhotel.co.uk

THE FRENCH HORN

Sonning-on-thames, Berkshire RG4 0TN

Tel: 01189 692204 **Fax:** 01189 442210

e-mail: TheFrenchHorn@Compuserve.com

THE SWAN AT STREATLEY

Streatley-on-thames, Berkshire RG8 9HR

Tel: 01491 878800 **Fax:** 01491 872554

e-mail: sales@swan-at-streatley.co.uk

Sir Christopher Wren's House Hotel

Thames Street, Windsor, Berkshire SL4 1PX

Tel: 01753 861354 **Fax:** 01753 860172

e-mail: reservations@wrensgroup.com

BERKSHIRE - WINDSOR

The Castle Hotel

High Street, Windsor, Berkshire SL4 1LJ

Tel: 0870 400 8300 **Fax:** 01753 830244

e-mail: castle@macdonald-hotels.co.uk

BIRMINGHAM

The Burlington Hotel

Burlington Arcade, 126 New Street, Birmingham, West Midlands B2 4JQ

Tel: 0121 643 9191 **Fax:** 0121 643 5075

e-mail: mail@burlingtonhotel.com

BIRMINGHAM

Hotel Du Vin & Bistro

Church Street, Birmingham B3 2NR

Tel: 0121 200 0600 **Fax:** 0121 236 0889

e-mail: info@birmingham.hotelduvin.com

BIRMINGHAM - WALMLEY

New Hall

Walmley Road, Royal Sutton Coldfield, West Midlands B76 1QX

Tel: 0121 378 2442 **Fax:** 0121 378 4637

e-mail: new-hall@thistle.co.uk

BRISTOL

Hotel Du Vin & Bistro

The Sugar House, Narrow Lewins Mead, Bristol BS1 2NU

Tel: 0117 925 5577 **Fax:** 0117 925 1199

e-mail: info@bristol.hotelduvin.com

BUCKINGHAMSHIRE - AYLESBURY

Hartwell House

Oxford Road, Nr Aylesbury, Buckinghamshire HP17 8NL

Tel: 01296 747444 **Fax:** 01296 747450

e-mail: info@hartwell–house.com

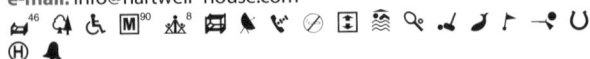

BUCKINGHAMSHIRE - AYLESBURY (WHITCHURCH)

The Priory Hotel

High Street, Whitchurch, Aylesbury, Buckinghamshire HP22 4JS

Tel: 01296 641239 **Fax:** 01296 641793

BUCKINGHAMSHIRE - HEATHROW

Stoke Park Club

Park Road, Stoke Poges, Buckinghamshire SL2 4PG

Tel: 01753 717171 **Fax:** 01753 717181

e-mail: info@stokeparkclub.com

BUCKINGHAMSHIRE - MAIDENHEAD (TAPLOW)

Taplow House Hotel

Berry Hill, Taplow, Nr Maidenhead, Buckinghamshire SL6 0DA

Tel: 01628 670056 **Fax:** 01628 773625

e-mail: taplow@wrensgroup.com

BUCKINGHAMSHIRE - MARLOW-ON-THAMES

Danesfield House Hotel And Spa

Henley Road, Marlow-on-thames, Buckinghamshire SL7 2EY

Tel: 01628 891010 **Fax:** 01628 890408

e-mail: sales@danesfieldhouse.co.uk

CAMBRIDGESHIRE - CAMBRIDGE

Hotel Felix

Whitehouse Lane, Huntingdon Road, Cambridge CB3 0LX

Tel: 01223 277977 **Fax:** 01223 277973

e-mail: info@hotelfelix.co.uk

CAMBRIDGESHIRE - CAMBRIDGE (MELBOURN)

MELBOURN BURY

Melbourn, Cambridgeshire, Nr Royston SG8 6DE

Tel: 01763 261151 **Fax:** 01763 262375

e-mail: melbournbury@biztobiz.co.uk

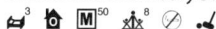

CAMBRIDGESHIRE - PETERBOROUGH (WANSFORD)

THE HAYCOCK

Wansford, Peterborough, Cambridgeshire PE8 6JA

Tel: 01780 782223 or 0800 9 177 877 **Fax:** 01780 783031

e-mail: haycock@arcadianhotels.co.uk

CAMBRIDGESHIRE - WISBECH (OUTWELL)

CROWN LODGE HOTEL

Downham Road, Outwell, Wisbech, Cambridgeshire PE14 8SE

Tel: 01945 773391 **Fax:** 01945 772668

e-mail: crownlodgehotel@hotmail.com

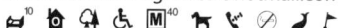

CHESHIRE - ALDERLEY EDGE

THE ALDERLEY EDGE HOTEL

Macclesfield Road, Alderley Edge, Cheshire SK9 7BJ

Tel: 01625 583033 **Fax:** 01625 586343

e-mail: sales@alderley–edge–hotel.co.uk

CHESHIRE - CHESTER

GREEN BOUGH HOTEL

60 Hoole Road, Chester, Cheshire CH2 3NL

Tel: 01244 326241 **Fax:** 01244 326265

e-mail: luxury@greenbough.co.uk

CHESHIRE - CHESTER

THE CHESTER CRABWALL MANOR

Parkgate Road, Mollington, Chester, Cheshire CH1 6NE

Tel: 01244 851666 **Fax:** 01244 851400

e-mail: crabwallmanor@marstonhotels.com

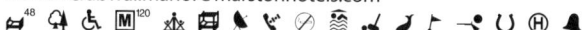

Frogg Manor Hotel & Restaurant

Fullers Moor, Nantwich Road, Broxton, Chester CH3 9JH

Tel: 01829 782629 **Fax:** 01829 782459

e-mail: info@froggmanorhotel.co.uk

Broxton Hall Country House Hotel

Whitchurch Road, Broxton, Chester, Cheshire CH3 9JS

Tel: 01829 782321 **Fax:** 01829 782330

e-mail: reservation@broxtonhall.co.uk

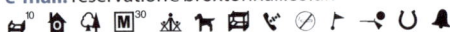

Brook Meadow Hotel

Heath Lane, Childer Thornton, Cheshire CH66 7NS

Tel: 0151 339 9350 **Fax:** 0151 347 4221

e-mail: brookmeadowhotel@btconnect.com

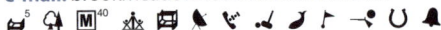

Nunsmere Hall

Tarporley Road, Oakmere, Northwich, Cheshire CW8 2ES

Tel: 01606 889100 **Fax:** 01606 889055

e-mail: reservations@nunsmere.co.uk

Rowton Hall Hotel

Whitchurch Road, Rowton, Chester, Cheshire CH3 6AD

Tel: 01244 335262 **Fax:** 01244 335464

e-mail: rowtonhall@rowtonhall.co.uk

Willington Hall Hotel

Willington, Nr Tarporley, Cheshire CW6 0NB

Tel: 01829 752321 **Fax:** 01829 752596

e-mail: enquiries@willingtonhall.co.uk

CREWE HALL

Weston Road, Crewe, Cheshire CW1 6UZ

Tel: 01270 253333 **Fax:** 01270 253322

e-mail: info@crewehall.com

MERE COURT HOTEL

Warrington Road, Mere, Knutsford, Cheshire WA16 0RW

Tel: 01565 831000 **Fax:** 01565 831001

e-mail: sales@merecourt.co.uk

THE STANNEYLANDS HOTEL

Stanneylands Road, Wilmslow, Cheshire SK9 4EY

Tel: 01625 525225 **Fax:** 01625 537282

e-mail: sales@stanneylandshotel.co.uk

ROOKERY HALL

Worleston, Nantwich, Nr Chester, Cheshire CW5 6DQ

Tel: 01270 610016 or 0800 9 177 877 **Fax:** 01270 626027

e-mail: rookery@arcadianhotels.co.uk

THE NARE HOTEL

Carne Beach, Veryan-in-roseland, Truro, Cornwall TR2 5PF

Tel: 01872 501111 **Fax:** 01872 501856

e-mail: office@narehotel.co.uk

PENMERE MANOR

Mongleath Road, Falmouth, Cornwall TR11 4PN

Tel: 01326 211411 **Fax:** 01326 317588

e-mail: reservations@penmere.co.uk

THE GREENBANK HOTEL

Harbourside, Falmouth, Cornwall TR11 2SR

Tel: 01326 312440 **Fax:** 01326 211362

e-mail: sales@greenbank-hotel.com

BUDOCK VEAN - THE HOTEL ON THE RIVER

Near Helford Passage, Mawnan Smith, Falmouth, Cornwall TR11 5LG

Tel: reservations 01326 252100 **Fax:** 01326 250892

e-mail: relax@budockvean.co.uk

MEUDON HOTEL

Mawnan Smith, Nr Falmouth, Cornwall TR11 5HT

Tel: 01326 250541 **Fax:** 01326 250543

e-mail: wecare@meudon.co.uk

TRELAWNE HOTEL – THE HUTCHES RESTAURANT

Mawnan Smith, Nr Falmouth, Cornwall TR11 5HS

Tel: 01326 250226 **Fax:** 01326 250909

e-mail:

FOWEY HALL HOTEL & RESTAURANT

Hanson Drive, Fowey, Cornwall PL23 1ET

Tel: 01726 833866 **Fax:** 01726 834100

e-mail: info@foweyhall.com

THE OLD QUAY HOUSE HOTEL

28 Fore Street, Fowey, Cornwall PL23 1AQ

Tel: 01726 833302 **Fax:** 01726 833668

e-mail: info@theoldquayhouse.com

Cormorant On The River, Hotel & Riverside Restaurant

Golant By Fowey, Cornwall PL23 1LL

Tel: 01726 833426

e-mail: relax@cormoranthotels.co.uk

St Martin's On The Isle

St. Martin's, Isles Of Scilly, Cornwall TR25 0QW

Tel: 01720 422090 **Fax:** 01720 422298

e-mail: stay@stmartinshotel.co.uk

Hell Bay

Bryher, Isles Of Scilly, Cornwall TR23 0PR

Tel: 01720 422947 **Fax:** 01720 423004

e-mail: contactus@hellbay.co.uk

Trehaven Manor Hotel

Station Road, Looe, Cornwall PL13 1HN

Tel: 01503 262028 **Fax:** 01503 265613

e-mail: enquiries@trehavenhotel.co.uk

Trevalsa Court Hotel

School Hill, Mevagissey, St Austell, Cornwall PL26 6TH

Tel: 01726 842468 **Fax:** 01726 844482

e-mail: trevalsacourthotel@yahoo.co.uk

Higher Faugan Country House Hotel

Chywoone Hill, Newlyn, Cornwall TR18 5NS

Tel: 01736 362076 **Fax:** 01736 351648

e-mail: reception@higherfaugan-hotel.co.uk

TREGLOS HOTEL

Constantine Bay, Nr Padstow, Cornwall PL28 8JH

Tel: 01841 520727 **Fax:** 01841 521163

e-mail: enquiries@treglos-hotel.co.uk

JUBILEE INN

Pelynt, Nr Looe, Cornwall PL13 2JZ

Tel: 01503 220312 **Fax:** 01503 220920

e-mail: rickard@jubileeinn.com

TALLAND BAY HOTEL

Talland-by-looe, Cornwall PL13 2JB

Tel: 01503 272667 **Fax:** 01503 272940

e-mail: tallandbay@aol.com

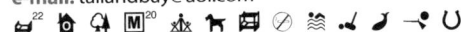

THE LUGGER HOTEL

Portloe, Nr Truro, Cornwall TR2 5RD

Tel: 01872 501322 **Fax:** 01872 501691

e-mail: office@luggerhotel.com

ROSE-IN-VALE COUNTRY HOUSE HOTEL

Mithian, St Agnes, Cornwall TR5 0QD

Tel: 01872 552202 **Fax:** 01872 552700

e-mail: reception@rose-in-vale-hotel.co.uk

BOSCUNDLE MANOR

Tregrehan, St. Austell, Cornwall PL25 3RL

Tel: 01726 813557 **Fax:** 01726 814997

e-mail: stay@boscundlemanor.co.uk

HUSTYNS HOTEL & LEISURE CLUB

St. Breock Downs, Wadebridge, Cornwall PL27 7LG

Tel: 01208 893700 **Fax:** 01208 893701

e-mail: reception@hustyns.com

THE GARRACK HOTEL & RESTAURANT

Burthallan Lane, St Ives, Cornwall TR26 3AA

Tel: 01736 796199 **Fax:** 01736 798955

e-mail: garrack@accuk.co.uk

THE COUNTRYMAN AT TRINK HOTEL

Old Coach Road, St Ives, Cornwall TR26 3JQ

Tel: 01736 797571 **Fax:** 01736 797571

e-mail: enquiries@the–countryman–hotel–stives.co.uk

THE WELL HOUSE

St Keyne, Liskeard, Cornwall PL14 4RN

Tel: 01579 342001 **Fax:** 01579 343891

e-mail: enquiries@wellhouse.co.uk

THE ROSEVINE HOTEL

Porthcurnick Beach, Portscatho, St Mawes, Truro, Cornwall TR2 5EW

Tel: 01872 580206 **Fax:** 01872 580230

e-mail: info@rosevine.co.uk

THE PORT WILLIAM

Trebarwith Strand, Nr Tintagel, Cornwall PL34 0HB

Tel: 01840 770230 **Fax:** 01840 770936

e-mail: william@eurobell.co.uk

CORNWALL - WADEBRIDGE (HELLAND BRIDGE)

TREDETHY HOUSE

Helland Bridge, Bodmin, Cornwall PL30 4QS

Tel: 01208 841262 **Fax:** 01208 841707

e-mail: amandarose@tredethyhouse.co.uk

CORNWALL - WADEBRIDGE (WASHAWAY)

TREHELLAS HOUSE HOTEL & RESTAURANT

Washaway, Bodmin, Cornwall PL30 3AD

Tel: 01208 72700 **Fax:** 01208 73336

e-mail: trehellashouse@aol.com

CUMBRIA - ALSTON

LOVELADY SHIELD COUNTRY HOUSE HOTEL

Nenthead Road, Alston, Cumbria CA9 3LF

Tel: 01434 381203 **Fax:** 01434 381515

e-mail: enquiries@lovelady.co.uk

CUMBRIA - AMBLESIDE

HOLBECK GHYLL COUNTRY HOUSE HOTEL

Holbeck Lane, Windermere, Cumbria LA23 1LU

Tel: 015394 32375 **Fax:** 015394 34743

e-mail: stay@holbeckghyll.com

CUMBRIA - AMBLESIDE

ROTHAY MANOR

Rothay Bridge, Ambleside, Cumbria LA22 0EH

Tel: 015394 33605 **Fax:** 015394 33607

e-mail: hotel@rothaymanor.co.uk

CUMBRIA - AMBLESIDE

THE SAMLING

Ambleside Road, Windermere, Cumbria LA23 1LR

Tel: 015394 31922 **Fax:** 015394 30400

e-mail: info@thesamling.com

GREY FRIAR LODGE

Clappersgate, Ambleside, Cumbria LA22 9NE

Tel: 015394 33158 **Fax:** 015394 33158

e-mail: greyfriar@veen.freeserve.co.uk

NANNY BROW COUNTRY HOUSE HOTEL & RESTAURANT

Clappersgate, Ambleside, Cumbria LA22 9NF

Tel: 015394 32036 **Fax:** 015394 32450

e-mail: reservations@nannybrow.co.uk

APPLEBY MANOR COUNTRY HOUSE HOTEL

Roman Road, Appleby-in-westmorland, Cumbria CA16 6JB

Tel: 017683 51571 **Fax:** 017683 52888

e-mail: reception@applebymanor.co.uk

TUFTON ARMS HOTEL

Market Square, Appleby-in-westmorland, Cumbria CA16 6XA

Tel: 017683 51593 **Fax:** 017683 52761

e-mail: info@tuftonarmshotel.co.uk

FARLAM HALL HOTEL

Brampton, Cumbria CA8 2NG

Tel: 016977 46234 **Fax:** 016977 46683

e-mail: farlamhall@dial.pipex.com

UNDERWOOD

The Hill, Millom, Cumbria LA18 5EZ

Tel: 01229 771116 **Fax:** 01229 719900

e-mail: enquiries@underwoodhouse.co.uk

CROSBY LODGE COUNTRY HOUSE HOTEL

High Crosby, Crosby-on-eden, Carlisle, Cumbria CA6 4QZ

Tel: 01228 573618 **Fax:** 01228 573428

e-mail: info@crosbylodge.co.uk

THE TARN END HOUSE HOTEL

Talkin Tarn, Brampton, Cumbria CA8 1LS

Tel: 016977 2340 **Fax:** 016977 2089

e-mail:

GRAYTHWAITE MANOR

Fernhill Road, Grange-over-sands, Cumbria LA11 7JE

Tel: 015395 32001 **Fax:** 015395 35549

e-mail: sales@graythwaitemanor.co.uk

THE WORDSWORTH HOTEL

Grasmere, Cumbria LA22 9SW

Tel: 015394 35592 **Fax:** 015394 35765

e-mail: enquiry@wordsworth–grasmere.co.uk

WHITE MOSS HOUSE

Rydal Water, Grasmere, Cumbria LA22 9SE

Tel: 015394 35295 **Fax:** 015394 35516

e-mail: dixon@whitemoss.com

THE QUEEN'S HEAD HOTEL

Main Street, Hawkshead, Cumbria LA22 0NS

Tel: 015394 36271 **Fax:** 015394 36722

e-mail: enquiries@queensheadhotel.co.uk

Sawrey House Country Hotel & Restaurant

Near Sawrey, Hawkshead, Ambleside, Cumbria LA22 0LF

Tel: 015394 36387 **Fax:** 015394 36010

e-mail: enquiries@sawrey–house.com

The Derwentwater Hotel

Portinscale, Keswick, Cumbria CA12 5RE

Tel: 017687 72538 **Fax:** 017687 71002

e-mail: info@derwentwater–hotel.co.uk

The Leathes Head

Borrowdale, Keswick, Cumbria CA12 5UY

Tel: 017687 77247 **Fax:** 017687 77363

e-mail: enq@leatheshead.co.uk

The Borrowdale Gates Country House Hotel

Grange-in-borrowdale, Keswick, Cumbria CA12 5UQ

Tel: 017687 77204 **Fax:** 017687 77254

e-mail: hotel@borrowdale-gates.com

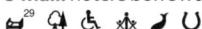

Dale Head Hall Lakeside Hotel

Thirlmere, Keswick, Cumbria CA12 4TN

Tel: 017687 72478 **Fax:** 017687 71070

e-mail: onthelakeside@daleheadhall.info

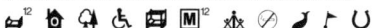

Swinside Lodge Hotel

Grange Road, Newlands, Keswick, Cumbria CA12 5UE

Tel: 017687 72948 **Fax:** 017687 72948

e-mail: info@swinsidelodge-hotel.co.uk

HIPPING HALL

Cowan Bridge, Kirkby Lonsdale, Cumbria LA6 2JJ
Tel: 015242 71187 **Fax:** 015242 72452
e-mail: hippinghal@aol.com

SHARROW BAY COUNTRY HOUSE HOTEL

Howtown, Lake Ullswater, Penrith, Cumbria CA10 2LZ
Tel: 017684 86301/86483 **Fax:** 017684 86349
e-mail: enquiries@sharrow–bay.com

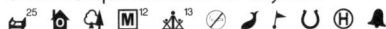

THE INN ON THE LAKE

Lake Ullswater, Glenridding, Cumbria CA11 0PE
Tel: 017684 82444 **Fax:** 017684 82303
e-mail: info@innonthelakeullswater.co.uk

RAMPSBECK COUNTRY HOUSE HOTEL

Watermillock, Lake Ullswater, Nr Penrith, Cumbria CA11 0LP
Tel: 017684 86442 **Fax:** 017684 86688
e-mail: enquiries@rampbeck.fsnet.co.uk

TEMPLE SOWERBY HOUSE HOTEL

Temple Sowerby, Penrith, Cumbria CA10 1RZ
Tel: 017683 61578 **Fax:** 017683 61958
e-mail: stay@temple–sowerby.com

GILPIN LODGE

Crook Road, Near Windermere, Cumbria LA23 3NE
Tel: 015394 88818 **Fax:** 015394 88058
e-mail: hotel@gilpin-lodge.co.uk

Langdale Chase

Windermere, Cumbria LA23 1LW

Tel: 015394 32201 **Fax:** 015394 32604

e-mail: sales@langdalechase.co.uk

Miller Howe

Rayrigg Road, Windermere, Cumbria LA23 1EY

Tel: 015394 42536 **Fax:** 015394 45664

e-mail: lakeview@millerhowe.com

Storrs Hall

Windermere, Cumbria LA23 3LG

Tel: 015394 47111 **Fax:** 015394 47555

e-mail: reception@storrshall.com

Linthwaite House Hotel

Crook Road, Bowness-on-windermere, Cumbria LA23 3JA

Tel: 015394 88600 **Fax:** 015394 88601

e-mail: admin@linthwaite.com

Fayrer Garden House Hotel

Lyth Valley Road, Bowness-on-windermere, Cumbria LA23 3JP

Tel: 015394 88195 **Fax:** 015394 45986

e-mail: lakescene@fayrergarden.com

Lakeside Hotel On Lake Windermere

Lakeside, Newby Bridge, Cumbria LA12 8AT

Tel: 08701 541586 **Fax:** 015395 31699

e-mail: sales@lakesidehotel.co.uk

SPA

Broadoaks Country House

Bridge Lane, Troutbeck, Windermere, Cumbria LA23 1LA

Tel: 01539 445566 **Fax:** 01539 488766

e-mail: trev@broakoaksf9.co.uk

Callow Hall

Mappleton Road, Ashbourne, Derbyshire DE6 2AA

Tel: 01335 300900 **Fax:** 01335 300512

e-mail: stay@callowhall.co.uk

The Izaak Walton Hotel

Dovedale, Near Ashbourne, Derbyshire DE6 2AY

Tel: 01335 350555 **Fax:** 01335 350539

e-mail: reception@izaakwaltonhotel.com

Riverside House

Ashford-in-the-water, Nr Bakewell, Derbyshire DE45 1QF

Tel: 01629 814275 **Fax:** 01629 812873

e-mail: riversidehouse@enta.net

Hassop Hall

Hassop, Nr Bakewell, Derbyshire DE45 1NS

Tel: 01629 640488 **Fax:** 01629 640577

e-mail: hassophallhotel@btinternet.com

East Lodge Country House Hotel

Rowsley, Nr Matlock, Derbyshire DE4 2EF

Tel: 01629 734474 **Fax:** 01629 733949

e-mail: info@eastlodge.com

DERBYSHIRE - BAKEWELL (ROWSLEY)

THE PEACOCK INN

Rowsley, Nr. Matlock, Derbyshire DE4 2EB

Tel: 01629 733518 **Fax:** 01629 732671

e-mail: jpeacock.gm@jarvis.co.uk

DERBYSHIRE - BASLOW

CAVENDISH HOTEL

Baslow, Derbyshire DE45 1SP

Tel: 01246 582311 **Fax:** 01246 582312

e-mail: info@cavendish–hotel.net

DERBYSHIRE - BASLOW

FISCHER'S

Baslow Hall, Calver Road, Baslow, Derbyshire DE45 1RR

Tel: 01246 583259 **Fax:** 01246 583818

e-mail: m.s@fischers–baslowhall.co.uk

DERBYSHIRE - BELPER

DANNAH FARM COUNTRY HOUSE

Bowman's Lane, Shottle, Nr Belper, Derbyshire DE56 2DR

Tel: 01773 550273/550630 **Fax:** 01773 550590

e-mail: reservations@dannah.demon.co.uk

DERBYSHIRE - BIGGIN-BY-HARTINGTON

BIGGIN HALL

Biggin-by-hartington, Buxton, Derbyshire SK17 0DH

Tel: 01298 84451 **Fax:** 01298 84681

e-mail: enquiries@bigginhall.co.uk

DERBYSHIRE - BURTON UPON TRENT (SUDBURY)

BOAR'S HEAD HOTEL

Lichfield Road, Sudbury, Derbyshire DE6 5GX

Tel: 01283 820344 **Fax:** 01283 820075

e-mail:

The Lee Wood Hotel & Restaurant

The Park, Buxton, Derbyshire SK17 6TQ

Tel: 01298 23002 **Fax:** 01298 23228

e-mail: leewoodhotel@btinternet.com

Buckingham's Hotel & Restaurant With One Table

85 Newbold Road, Chesterfield, Derbyshire S41 7PU

Tel: 01246 201041 **Fax:** 01246 550059

e-mail: info@buckinghams–table.com

Ringwood Hall Hotel

Ringwood Road, Brimington, Chesterfield, Derbyshire S43 1DQ

Tel: 01246 280077 **Fax:** 01246 472241

Littleover Lodge Hotel

222 Rykneld Road, Littleover, Derby, Derbyshire DE23 7AN

Tel: 01332 510161 **Fax:** 01332 514010

e-mail:

Risley Hall Country House Hotel

Derby Road, Risley, Derbyshire DE72 3SS

Tel: 0115 939 9000 **Fax:** 0115 939 7766

e-mail: johansens@risleyhallhotel.co.uk

The Chequers Inn

Froggatt Edge, Hope Valley, Derbyshire S32 3ZJ

Tel: 01433 630231 **Fax:** 01433 631072

e-mail: info@chequers-froggatt.com

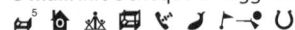

THE WIND IN THE WILLOWS

Derbyshire Level, Glossop, Derbyshire SK13 7PT

Tel: 01457 868001 **Fax:** 01457 853354

e-mail: info@windinthewillows.co.uk

THE MAYNARD ARMS

Main Road, Grindleford, Derbyshire S32 2HE

Tel: 01433 630321 **Fax:** 01433 630445

e-mail: info@maynardarms.co.uk

THE GEORGE AT HATHERSAGE

Main Road, Hathersage, Derbyshire S32 1BB

Tel: 01433 650436 **Fax:** 01433 650099

e-mail: info@george-hotel.net

THE PLOUGH INN

Leadmill Bridge, Hathersage, Derbyshire S30 1BA

Tel: 01433 650319 **Fax:** 01433 651049

e-mail: theploughinn@leadmillbridge.fsnet.co.uk

SANTO'S HIGHAM FARM

Main Road, Higham, Derbyshire DE55 6EH

Tel: 01773 833812/3/4 **Fax:** 01773 520525

e-mail: reception@santoshighamfarm.demon.co.uk

RIBER HALL

Matlock, Derbyshire DE4 5JU

Tel: 01629 582795 **Fax:** 01629 580475

e-mail: info@riber-hall.co.uk

YEOLDON HOUSE HOTEL

Durrant Lane, Northam, Nr Bideford EX39 2RL

Tel: 01237 474400 **Fax:** 01237 476618

e-mail: yeoldonhousehotel@aol.com

THE EDGEMOOR

Haytor Road, Bovey Tracey, South Devon TQ13 9LE

Tel: 01626 832466 **Fax:** 01626 834760

e-mail: edgemoor@btinternet.com

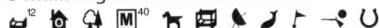

NORTHCOTE MANOR COUNTRY HOUSE HOTEL

Burrington, Umberleigh, Devon EX37 9LZ

Tel: 01769 560501 **Fax:** 01769 560770

e-mail: rest@northcotemanor.co.uk

GIDLEIGH PARK

Chagford, Devon TQ13 8HH

Tel: 01647 432367 **Fax:** 01647 432574

e-mail: gidleighpark@gidleigh.co.uk

MILL END

Dartmoor National Park, Chagford, Devon TQ13 8JN

Tel: 01647 432282 **Fax:** 01647 433106

e-mail: millendhotel@talk21.com

THE NEW INN

Coleford, Crediton, Devon EX17 5BZ

Tel: 01363 84242 **Fax:** 01363 85044

e-mail: new–inn@reallyreal-group.com

DEVON - COMBE MARTIN

COULSWORTHY HOUSE

Combe Martin, Devon EX34 0PD

Tel: 01271 882813

e-mail: .coulsworthy@tiscali.co.uk

DEVON - ERMINGTON

PLANTATION HOUSE HOTEL & MATISSE RESTAURANT

Totnes Road, Ermington, Devon PL21 9NS

Tel: 01548 831100 **Fax:** 01548 831248

e-mail: enquiries@plantationhousehotel.com

DEVON - EXETER

HOTEL BARCELONA

Magdalen Road, Exeter, Devon EX2 4HY

Tel: 01392 281000 **Fax:** 01392 281001

e-mail: info@hotelbarcelona–uk.com

DEVON - EXETER (DUNCHIDEOCK)

THE LORD HALDON COUNTRY HOTEL

Dunchideock, Nr Exeter, Devon EX6 7YF

Tel: 01392 832483 **Fax:** 01392 833765

e-mail: enquiries@lordhaldon.co.uk

DEVON - EXETER (HONITON)

COMBE HOUSE HOTEL & RESTAURANT

Gittisham, Honiton, Nr Exeter, Devon EX14 3AD

Tel: 01404 540400 **Fax:** 01404 46004

e-mail: stay@thishotel.com

DEVON - HAWKCHURCH (NR LYME REGIS)

FAIRWATER HEAD COUNTRY HOUSE HOTEL

Hawkchurch, Axminster, Devon EX13 5TX

Tel: 01297 678349 **Fax:** 01297 678459

e-mail: jclowe@btinternet.com

Home Farm Hotel

Wilmington, Nr Honiton, Devon EX14 9JR

Tel: 01404 831278 **Fax:** 01404 831411

e-mail: homefarmhotel@breathemail.net

Ilsington Country House Hotel

Ilsington Village, Near Newton Abbot, Devon TQ13 9RR

Tel: 01364 661452 **Fax:** 01364 661307

e-mail: hotel@ilsington.co.uk

The Arundell Arms

Lifton, Devon PL16 0AA

Tel: 01566 784666 **Fax:** 01566 784494

e-mail: reservations@arundellarms.com

The Rising Sun

Harbourside, Lynmouth, Devon EX35 6EG

Tel: 01598 753223 **Fax:** 01598 753480

e-mail: risingsunlynmouth@easynet.co.uk

Hewitt's - Villa Spaldi

North Walk, Lynton, Devon EX35 6HJ

Tel: 01598 752293 **Fax:** 01598 752489

e-mail: hewitts.hotel@talk21.com

Kitley House Hotel & Restaurant

The Kitley Estate, Yealmpton, Nr Plymouth, Devon PL8 2NW

Tel: 01752 881555 **Fax:** 01752 881667

e-mail: sales@kitleyhousehotel.com

KITLEY HOUSE HOTEL & RESTAURANT

The Kitley Estate, Yealmpton, Plymouth, Devon PL8 2NW
Tel: 01752 881555 **Fax:** 01752 881667
e-mail: sales@kitleyhousehotel.com

DEVON - SALCOMBE ESTUARY

BUCKLAND-TOUT-SAINTS

Goveton, Kingsbridge, Devon TQ7 2DS
Tel: 01548 853055 **Fax:** 01548 856261
e-mail: buckland@tout-saints.co.uk

DEVON - SALCOMBE (SOAR MILL COVE)

SOAR MILL COVE HOTEL

Soar Mill Cove, Salcombe, South Devon TQ7 3DS
Tel: 01548 561566 **Fax:** 01548 561223
e-mail: info@makepeacehotels.co.uk

DEVON - SALCOMBE (SOUTH SANDS)

THE TIDES REACH HOTEL

South Sands, Salcombe, Devon TQ8 8LJ
Tel: 01548 843466 **Fax:** 01548 843954
e-mail: enquire@tidesreach.com

DEVON - SAUNTON

PRESTON HOUSE & LITTLE'S RESTAURANT

Saunton, Braunton, North Devon EX33 1LG
Tel: 01271 890472 **Fax:** 01271 890555
e-mail: prestonhouse-saunton@zoom.co.uk

DEVON - SIDMOUTH

HOTEL RIVIERA

The Esplanade, Sidmouth, Devon EX10 8AY
Tel: 01395 515201 **Fax:** 01395 577775
e-mail: enquiries@hotelriviera.co.uk

Kingston House

Staverton, Totnes, Devon TQ9 6AR

Tel: 01803 762 235 **Fax:** 01803 762 444

e-mail: info@kingston–estate.co.uk

Browns Hotel, Wine Bar & Brasserie

80 West Street, Tavistock, Devon PL19 8AQ

Tel: 01822 618686 **Fax:** 01822 618646

e-mail: enquiries@brownsdevon.co.uk

The Palace Hotel

Babbacombe Road, Torquay, Devon TQ1 3TG

Tel: 01803 200200 **Fax:** 01803 299899

e-mail: info@palacetorquay.co.uk

Orestone Manor Hotel & Restaurant

Rockhouse Lane, Maidencombe, Torquay, Devon TQ1 4SX

Tel: 01803 328098 **Fax:** 01803 328336

e-mail: enquiries@orestone.co.uk

The Osborne Hotel & Langtry's Restaurant

Meadfoot Beach, Torquay, Devon TQ1 2LL

Tel: 01803 213311 **Fax:** 01803 296788

e-mail: enq@osborne-torquay.co.uk

The Sea Trout Inn

Staverton, Nr. Totnes, Devon TQ9 6PA

Tel: 01803 762274 **Fax:** 01803 762506

e-mail: enquiries@seatroutinn.com

DEVON - VIRGINSTOW (NR OKEHAMPTON)

Percy's Country Hotel & Restaurant

Coombeshead Estate, Virginstow, Devon EX21 5EA

Tel: 01409 211236 **Fax:** 01409 211275

e-mail: info@percys.co.uk

DEVON - WOOLACOMBE

Woolacombe Bay Hotel

South Street, Woolacombe, Devon EX34 7BN

Tel: 01271 870388 **Fax:** 01271 870613

e-mail: woolacombe.bayhotel@btinternet.com

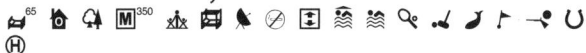

DEVON - WOOLACOMBE (MORTEHOE)

Watersmeet Hotel

Mortehoe, Woolacombe, Devon EX34 7EB

Tel: 01271 870333 **Fax:** 01271 870890

e-mail: info @watersmeethotel.co.uk

DORSET - BEAMINSTER

Bridge House Hotel

Prout Bridge, Beaminster, Dorset DT8 3AY

Tel: 01308 862200 **Fax:** 01308 863700

e-mail: enquiries@bridge–house.co.uk

DORSET - BOURNEMOUTH

Langtry Manor - Lovenest Of A King

Derby Road, East Cliff, Bournemouth, Dorset BH1 3QB

Tel: 01202 553887 **Fax:** 01202 290115

e-mail: lillie@langtrymanor.com

DORSET - BOURNEMOUTH

Norfolk Royale Hotel

Richmond Hill, Bournemouth, Dorset BH2 6EN

Tel: 01202 551521 **Fax:** 01202 299729

e-mail: norfolkroyale@englishrosehotels.co.uk

MENZIES EAST CLIFF COURT

East Overcliff Drive, Bournemouth, Dorset BH1 3DN

Tel: 01202 554545 **Fax:** 01202 557456

e-mail: eastcliffcourt@menzies-hotel.co.uk

THE DORMY

New Road, Ferndown, Near Bournemouth, Dorset BH22 8ES

Tel: 01202 872121 **Fax:** 01202 895388

e-mail: dormy@devere-hotels.com

THE MANOR HOTEL

West Bexington, Dorchester, Dorset DT2 9DF

Tel: 01308 897616 **Fax:** 01308 897035

e-mail: themanorhotel@bt.connect.com

YALBURY COTTAGE HOTEL

Lower Bockhampton, Dorchester, Dorset DT2 8PZ

Tel: 01305 262382 **Fax:** 01305 266412

e-mail: yalburycottage@aol.com

ACORN INN

Evershot, Dorset DT2 0JW

Tel: 01935 83228 **Fax:** 01935 83707

e-mail: stay@acorn-inn.co.uk

SUMMER LODGE

Summer Lane, Evershot, Dorset DT2 0JR

Tel: 01935 83424 **Fax:** 01935 83005

e-mail: reception@summerlodgehotel.com

THE EASTBURY HOTEL

Long Street, Sherborne, Dorset DT9 3BY

Tel: 01935 813131 **Fax:** 01935 817296

e-mail: eastbury.sherborne@virgin.net

PLUMBER MANOR

Sturminster Newton, Dorset DT10 2AF

Tel: 01258 472507 **Fax:** 01258 473370

e-mail: book@plumbermanor.com

THE PRIORY HOTEL

Church Green, Wareham, Dorset BH20 4ND

Tel: 01929 551666 **Fax:** 01929 554519

e-mail: reservations@theprioryhotel.co.uk

KEMPS COUNTRY HOTEL & RESTAURANT

East Stoke, Wareham, Dorset BH20 6AL

Tel: 01929 462563 **Fax:** 01929 405287

e-mail: kemps.hotel@lineone.net

MOONFLEET MANOR

Fleet, Weymouth, Dorset DT3 4ED

Tel: 01305 786948 **Fax:** 01305 774395

e-mail: info@moonfleetmanor.com

HEADLAM HALL

Headlam, Nr Gainford, Darlington, County Durham DL2 3HA

Tel: 01325 730238 **Fax:** 01325 730790

e-mail: admin@headlamhall.co.uk

Seaham Hall Hotel & Oriental Spa

Lord Byron's Walk, Seaham, Co Durham SR7 7AG

Tel: 0191 516 1400 **Fax:** 0191 516 1410

e-mail: reservations@seaham-hall.com

Grove House

Hamsterley Forest, Nr Bishop Auckland, Co Durham DL13 3NL

Tel: 01388 488203 **Fax:** 01388 488174

e-mail: grovehouse@dial.pipex.com

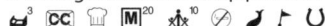

Horsley Hall

Eastgate, Nr Stanhope, Bishop Auckland, Co. Durham DL13 2LJ

Tel: 01388 517239 **Fax:** 01388 517608

e-mail: hotel@horsleyhall.co.uk

The Pump House Apartment

132 Church Street, Great Burstead, Essex CM11 2TR

Tel: 01277 656579 **Fax:** 01277 631160

e-mail: john.bayliss@willmottdixon.co.uk

The Cricketers

Clavering, Nr Saffron Walden, Essex CB11 4QT

Tel: 01799 550442 **Fax:** 01799 550882

e-mail: cricketers@lineone.net

Five Lakes Hotel, Golf, Country Club & Spa

Colchester Road, Tolleshunt Knights, Maldon, Essex CM9 8HX

Tel: 01621 868888 **Fax:** 01621 869696

e-mail: enquiries@fivelakes.co.uk

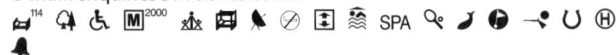

ESSEX - DEDHAM

MAISON TALBOOTH

Stratford Road, Dedham, Colchester, Essex CO7 6HN

Tel: 01206 322367 **Fax:** 01206 322752

e-mail: maison@talbooth.co.uk

ESSEX - GREAT CHESTERFORD (CAMBRIDGE)

THE CROWN HOUSE

Great Chesterford, Saffron Walden, Essex CB10 1NY

Tel: 01799 530515 / 530257 **Fax:** 01799 530683

e-mail:

ESSEX - HARWICH

THE PIER AT HARWICH

The Quay, Harwich, Essex CO12 3HH

Tel: 01255 241212 **Fax:** 01255 551922

e-mail: info@pieratharwich.co.uk

ESSEX - STOCK (NR CHELMSFORD)

GREENWOODS ESTATE

Stock Road, Stock, Essex CM4 9BE

Tel: 01277 829990 **Fax:** 01277 829899

e-mail: info@greenwoodsestate.com

GLOUCESTERSHIRE - BIBURY

THE SWAN HOTEL AT BIBURY

Bibury, Gloucestershire GL7 5NW

Tel: 01285 740695 **Fax:** 01285 740473

e-mail: swanhotl@swanhotel-cotswold.co.uk

GLOUCESTERSHIRE - BIBURY

BIBURY COURT

Bibury Court, Bibury, Gloucestershire GL7 5NT

Tel: 01285 740337 **Fax:** 01285 740660

e-mail: reservations@biburycourt.co.uk

Hotel Kandinsky

Bayshill Road, Montpellier, Cheltenham, Gloucestershire GL50 3AS

Tel: 01242 527788 **Fax:** 01242 226412

e-mail: info@hotelkandinsky.com

Hotel On The Park

Evesham Road, Cheltenham, Gloucestershire GL52 2AH

Tel: 01242 518898 **Fax:** 01242 511526

e-mail: stay@hotelonthepark.co.uk

The Green Dragon Inn

Cockleford, Nr Cowley, Cheltenham, Gloucester GL53 9NW

Tel: 01242 870271 **Fax:** 01242 870171

e-mail: green–dragon@buccaneer.co.uk

Charlton Kings Hotel

Charlton Kings, Cheltenham, Gloucestershire GL52 6UU

Tel: 01242 231061 **Fax:** 01242 241900

e-mail: enquiries@charltonkingshotel.co.uk

The Greenway

Shurdington, Cheltenham, Gloucestershire GL51 4UG

Tel: 01242 862352 **Fax:** 01242 862780

e-mail: greenway@btconnect.com

The White Hart Inn

High Street, Winchcombe, Nr. Cheltenham, Gloucestershire GL54 5LJ

Tel: 01242 602359 **Fax:** 01242 602703

e-mail: enquiries@the-white-hart-inn.com

CHARINGWORTH MANOR

Nr Chipping Campden, Gloucestershire GL55 6NS

Tel: 01386 593555 **Fax:** 01386 593353

e-mail: charingworthmanor@englishrosehotels.co.uk

COTSWOLD HOUSE

High Street, Chipping Campden, Gloucestershire GL55 6AN

Tel: 01386 840330 **Fax:** 01386 840310

e-mail: reception@cotswoldhouse.com

THE NOEL ARMS HOTEL

High Street, Chipping Campden, Gloucestershire GL55 6AT

Tel: 01386 840317 **Fax:** 01386 841136

e-mail: bookings@cotswold–inns–hotels.co.uk

THE MALT HOUSE

Broad Campden, Gloucestershire GL55 6UU

Tel: 01386 840295 **Fax:** 01386 841334

e-mail: nick@the–malt–house.freeserve.co.uk

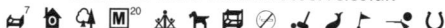

THE WILD DUCK INN

Drakes Island, Ewen, Cirencester, Gloucestershire GL7 6BY

Tel: 01285 770310 **Fax:** 01285 770924

e-mail: wduckinn@aol.com

THE NEW INN AT COLN

Coln St-aldwyns, Nr Cirencester, Gloucestershire GL7 5AN

Tel: 01285 750651 **Fax:** 01285 750657

e-mail: stay@new–inn.co.uk

THE BEAR OF RODBOROUGH

Rodborough Common, Stroud, Nr Cirencester, Gloucestershire GL5 5DE

Tel: 01453 878522 **Fax:** 01453 872523

e-mail: bookings@cotswold-inns-hotels.co.uk

LOWER SLAUGHTER MANOR

Lower Slaughter, Gloucestershire GL54 2HP

Tel: 01451 820456 **Fax:** 01451 822150

e-mail: lowsmanor@aol.com

WASHBOURNE COURT HOTEL

Lower Slaughter, Gloucestershire GL54 2HS

Tel: 01451 822143 **Fax:** 01451 821045

THE MANOR HOUSE HOTEL

Moreton-in-marsh, Gloucestershire GL56 0LJ

Tel: 01608 650501 **Fax:** 01608 651481

e-mail: bookings@cotswold–inns–hotels.co.uk

THREE CHOIRS VINEYARDS ESTATE

Newent, Gloucestershire GL18 1LS

Tel: 01531 890223 **Fax:** 01531 890877

e-mail: ts@threechoirs.com

THE PAINSWICK HOTEL

Kemps Lane, Painswick, Gloucestershire GL6 6YB

Tel: 01452 812160 **Fax:** 01452 814059

e-mail: Reservations@Painswickhotel.com

THE GRAPEVINE HOTEL

Sheep Street, Stow-on-the-wold, Gloucestershire GL54 1AU

Tel: 01451 830344 **Fax:** 01451 832278

e-mail: johansens@vines.co.uk

THE UNICORN HOTEL

Sheep Street, Stow-on-the-wold, Gloucestershire GL54 1HQ

Tel: 01451 830257 **Fax:** 01451 831090

e-mail: bookings@cotswold–inns–hotels.co.uk

WYCK HILL HOUSE

Wyck Hill, Stow-on-the Wold, Gloucestershire GL54 1HY

Tel: 01451 831936 **Fax:** 01451 832243

e-mail: wyckhill@wrensgroup.com

LORDS OF THE MANOR HOTEL

Upper Slaughter, Nr Bourton-on-the-water, Gloucestershire GL54 2JD

Tel: 01451 820243 **Fax:** 01451 820696

e-mail: lordsofthemanor@btinternet.com

CALCOT MANOR

Nr Tetbury, Gloucestershire GL8 8YJ

Tel: 01666 890391 **Fax:** 01666 890394

e-mail: reception@calcotmanor.co.uk

THE CLOSE HOTEL

Long Street, Tetbury, Gloucestershire GL8 8AQ

Tel: 01666 502272 **Fax:** 01666 504401

e-mail: reception@theclosehotel.co.uk

Corse Lawn House Hotel

Corse Lawn, Nr Tewkesbury, Gloucestershire GL19 4LZ

Tel: 01452 780479/771 **Fax:** 01452 780840

e-mail: hotel@corselawnhouse.u–net.com

Thornbury Castle

Thornbury, South Gloucestershire BS35 1HH

Tel: 01454 281182 **Fax:** 01454 416188

e-mail: thornburycastle@compuserve.com

Esseborne Manor

Hurstbourne Tarrant, Andover, Hampshire SP11 0ER

Tel: 01264 736444 **Fax:** 01264 736725

e-mail: esseborne@aol.com

Fifehead Manor

Middle Wallop, Stockbridge. Hampshire SO20 8EG

Tel: 01264 781565 **Fax:** 01264 781400

e-mail: fifeheadmanor@ukonline.co.uk

New Mill Restaurant

New Mill Road, Eversley, Hampshire RG27 0RA

Tel: 0118 973 2277 **Fax:** 0118 932 8780

e-mail: info@thenewmill.co.uk

Tylney Hall

Rotherwick, Hook, Hampshire RG27 9AZ

Tel: 01256 764881 **Fax:** 01256 768141

e-mail: reservations@tylneyhall.com

The Montagu Arms Hotel

Beaulieu, New Forest, Hampshire SO42 7ZL

Tel: 01590 612324   **Fax:** 01590 612188

e-mail: enquiries@montagu–arms.co.uk

The Master Builder's House

Buckler's Hard, Beaulieu, New Forest, Hampshire SO42 7XB

Tel: 01590 616253   **Fax:** 01590 616297

e-mail: res@themasterbuilders.co.uk

Careys Manor Hotel

Brockenhurst, New Forest, Hampshire SO42 7RH

Tel: 01590 623551   **Fax:** 01590 622799

e-mail: info@careysmanor.com

New Park Manor

Lyndhurst Road, Brockenhurst, New Forest, Hampshire SO42 7QH

Tel: 01590 623467   **Fax:** 01590 622268

e-mail: enquiries@newparkmanorhotel.co.uk

Rhinefield House Hotel

Rhinefield Road, Brockenhurst, New Forest, Hampshire SO42 7QB

Tel: 01590 622922   **Fax:** 01590 622800

e-mail: info@rhinefieldhousehotel.co.uk

Thatched Cottage Hotel & Restaurant

16 Brookley Road, Brockenhurst, New Forest, Hampshire SO42 7RR

Tel: 01590 623090   **Fax:** 01590 623479

e-mail: sales@thatchedcottage.co.uk

WHITLEY RIDGE COUNTRY HOUSE HOTEL

Beaulieu Road, Brockenhurst, New Forest, Hampshire SO42 7QL

Tel: 01590 622354 **Fax:** 01590 622856

e-mail: whitleyridge@brockenhurst.co.uk

OLD THORNS HOTEL, GOLF & COUNTRY CLUB

Longmoor Road, Griggs Green, Liphook, Hampshire GU30 7PE

Tel: 01428 724555 **Fax:** 01428 725036

e-mail: info@oldthorns.com

PASSFORD HOUSE HOTEL

Mount Pleasant Lane, Lymington, Hampshire SO41 8LS

Tel: 01590 682398 **Fax:** 01590 683494

e-mail: sales@passfordhousehotel.co.uk

STANWELL HOUSE

High Street, Lymington, New Forest, Hampshire SO41 9AA

Tel: 01590 677123 **Fax:** 01590 677756

e-mail: sales@stanwellhousehotel.co.uk

GORDLETON MILL INN

Silver Street, Hordle, Nr Lymington, New Forest, Hampshire SO41 6DJ

Tel: 01590 682219 **Fax:** 01590 683073

e-mail: bookings@gordleton-mill.co.uk

WESTOVER HALL

Park Lane, Milford-on-sea, Hampshire SO41 0PT

Tel: 01590 643044 **Fax:** 01590 644490

e-mail: info@westoverhallhotel.com

THE NURSE'S COTTAGE

Station Road, Sway, Lymington, Hampshire SO41 6BA

Tel: 01590 683402 **Fax:** 01590 683402

e-mail: nurses.cottage@lineone.net

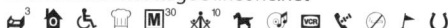

LE POUSSIN AT PARKHILL

Beaulieu Road, Lyndhurst, New Forest, Hampshire SO43 7FZ

Tel: 023 8028 2944 **Fax:** 023 8028 3268

e-mail: sales@lepoussinatparkhill.co.uk

CHEWTON GLEN

New Milton, Hampshire BH25 6QS

Tel: 01425 275341 **Fax:** 01425 272310

e-mail: reservations@chewtonglen.com

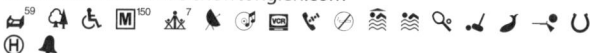

LANGRISH HOUSE

Langrish, Nr Petersfield, Hampshire GU32 1RN

Tel: 01730 266941 **Fax:** 01730 260543

e-mail: frontdesk@langrishhouse.co.uk

HOTEL DU VIN & BISTRO

Southgate Street, Winchester, Hampshire SO23 9EF

Tel: 01962 841414 **Fax:** 01962 842458

e-mail: info@tunbridgewells.hotelduvin.com

LAINSTON HOUSE HOTEL

Sparsholt, Winchester, Hampshire SO21 2LT

Tel: 01962 863588 **Fax:** 01962 776672

e-mail: enquiries@lainstonhouse.com

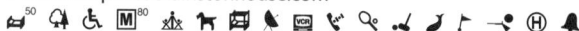

HEREFORDSHIRE - ABERGAVENNY (WALTERSTONE)

ALLT-YR-YNYS HOTEL

Walterstone, Nr Abergavenny Herefordshire HR2 0DU

Tel: 01873 890307 **Fax:** 01873 890539

e-mail: allthotel@compuserve.com

HEREFORDSHIRE - HEREFORD (ULLINGSWICK)

THE STEPPES

Ullingswick, Nr Hereford, Herefordshire HR1 3JG

Tel: 01432 820424 **Fax:** 01432 820042

e-mail: info@steppeshotel.co.uk

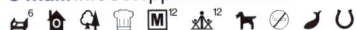

HEREFORDSHIRE - LEDBURY

THE FEATHERS HOTEL

High Street, Ledbury, Herefordshire HR8 1DS

Tel: 01531 635266 **Fax:** 01531 638955

e-mail: mary@feathers–ledbury.co.uk

HEREFORDSHIRE - ROSS-ON-WYE

THE CHASE HOTEL

Gloucester Road, Ross-on-wye, Herefordshire HR9 5LH

Tel: 01989 763161 **Fax:** 01989 768330

e-mail: info@chasehotel.co.uk

HEREFORDSHIRE - ROSS-ON-WYE

WILTON COURT HOTEL

Wilton, Ross-on-wye, Herefordshire HR9 6AQ

Tel: +44 (0)1989 562569 **Fax:** +44 (0)1989 768460

e-mail: info@wiltoncourthotel.com

HEREFORDSHIRE - ROSS-ON-WYE (GLEWSTONE)

GLEWSTONE COURT

Nr Ross-on-wye, Herefordshire HR9 6AW

Tel: 01989 770367 **Fax:** 01989 770282

e-mail: glewstone@aol.com

Down Hall Country House Hotel

Hatfield Heath, Nr Bishop's Stortford, Hertfordshire CM22 7AS

Tel: 01279 731441 **Fax:** 01279 730416

e-mail: reservations@downhall.co.uk

Sopwell House Hotel, Country Club & Spa

Cottonmill Lane, Sopwell, St Albans, Hertfordshire AL1 2HQ

Tel: 01727 864477 **Fax:** 01727 844741/845636

e-mail: enquiries@sopwellhouse.co.uk

St Michael's Manor

St Michael's Village, Fishpool Street, St Albans, Hertfordshire AL3 4RY

Tel: 01727 864444 **Fax:** 01727 848909

e-mail: smmanor@globalnet.co.uk

Redcoats Farmhouse Hotel And Restaurant

Redcoats Green, Near Hitchin, Herts SG4 7JR

Tel: 01438 729500 **Fax:** 01438 723322

e-mail: sales@redcoats.co.uk

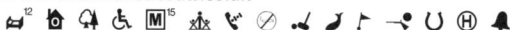

Pendley Manor Hotel & Conference Centre

Cow Lane, Tring, Hertfordshire HP23 5QY

Tel: 01442 891891 **Fax:** 01442 890687

e-mail: sales@pendley–manor.co.uk

Hanbury Manor

Ware, Hertfordshire SG12 0SD

Tel: 01920 487722 **Fax:** 01920 487692

e-mail: conferenceandevents.hanburymanor@marriotthotels.co.uk

ISLE OF WIGHT - SEAVIEW

THE PRIORY BAY HOTEL

Priory Drive, Seaview, Isle Of Wight PO34 5BU

Tel: 01983 613146 **Fax:** 01983 616539

e-mail: reception@priorybay.co.uk

ISLE OF WIGHT - (SHANKLIN)

RYLSTONE MANOR

Rylstone Gardens, Shanklin, Isle Of Wight PO37 6RE

Tel: 01983 862806 **Fax:** 01983 862806

e-mail: rylstone@dialstart.net

ISLE OF WIGHT - YARMOUTH

THE GEORGE HOTEL

Quay Street, Yarmouth, Isle Of Wight PO41 0PE

Tel: 01983 760331 **Fax:** 01983 760425

e-mail: res@thegeorge.co.uk

KENT - ASHFORD (BOUGHTON LEES)

EASTWELL MANOR

Boughton Lees, Nr Ashford, Kent TN25 4HR

Tel: 01233 213000 **Fax:** 01233 635530

e-mail: eastwell@marstonhotels.com

KENT - CANTERBURY (CHARTHAM HATCH)

HOWFIELD MANOR

Chartham Hatch, Nr Canterbury, Kent CT4 7HQ

Tel: 01227 738294 **Fax:** 01227 731535

e-mail: enquiries@howfield.invictanet.co.uk

KENT - CRANBROOK

THE GEORGE HOTEL

Stone Street, Cranbrook, Kent TN17 3HE

Tel: 01580 713348 **Fax:** 01580 715532

e-mail: georgecranbrook@aol.com

KENT - DARTFORD (WILMINGTON)

Rowhill Grange Hotel And Spa

Wilmington, Dartford, Kent DA2 7QH

Tel: 01322 615136 **Fax:** 01322 615137

e-mail: admin@rowhillgrange.com

KENT - DOVER (WEST CLIFFE)

Wallett's Court

West Cliffe, St Margaret's-at-cliffe, Dover, Kent CT15 6EW

Tel: 01304 852424 **Fax:** 01304 853430

e-mail: wc@wallettscourt.com

KENT - ELHAM (NR CANTERBURY)

The Abbot's Fireside Hotel

High Street, Elham, Near Canterbury, Kent CT4 6TD

Tel: 01303 840265 **Fax:** 01303 840852

e-mail: info@abbotsfireside.com

KENT - MAIDSTONE (LENHAM)

Chilston Park

Sandway, Lenham, Nr Maidstone, Kent ME17 2BE

Tel: 01622 859803 **Fax:** 01622 858588

e-mail: chilstonpark@arcadianhotels.co.uk

KENT - MAIDSTONE (RINGLESTONE)

Ringlestone Inn and Farmhouse Hotel

Twixt Harrietsham And Wormshill, Nr Maidstone, Kent ME17 1NX

Tel: 01622 859900 **Fax:** 01622 859966

e-mail: bookings@ringlestone.com

KENT - NEW ROMNEY (LITTLESTONE)

Romney Bay House

Coast Road, Littlestone, New Romney, Kent TN28 8QY

Tel: 01797 364747 **Fax:** 01797 367156

e-mail:

....

HOTEL DU VIN & BISTRO

Crescent Road, Royal Tunbridge Wells, Kent TN1 2LY

Tel: 01892 526455 **Fax:** 01892 512044

e-mail: reception@tunbridgewells.hotelduvin.com

....

THE SPA HOTEL

Mount Ephraim, Royal Tunbridge Wells, Kent TN4 8XJ

Tel: 01892 520331 **Fax:** 01892 510575

e-mail: reservations@spahotel.co.uk

....

ASTLEY BANK HOTEL & CONFERENCE CENTRE

Bolton Road, Darwen, Lancashire BB3 2QB

Tel: 01254 777700 **Fax:** 01254 777707

e-mail: sales@astleybank.co.uk

....

NORTHCOTE MANOR

Northcote Road, Langho, Blackburn BB6 8BE

Tel: 01254 240555 **Fax:** 01254 246568

e-mail: sales@northcotemanor.com

....

THE GIBBON BRIDGE HOTEL

Nr Chipping, Forest Of Bowland, Lancashire PR3 2TQ

Tel: 01995 61456 **Fax:** 01995 61277

e-mail: reception@gibbon–bridge.co.uk

....

YE HORN'S INN

Horn's Lane, Goosnargh, Nr Preston, Lancashire PR3 2FJ

Tel: 01772 865230 **Fax:** 01772 864299

e-mail: enquiries@yehornsinn.co.uk

TREE TOPS COUNTRY HOUSE RESTAURANT & HOTEL

Southport Old Road, Formby, Nr Southport, Lancashire L37 0AB

Tel: 01704 572430 **Fax:** 01704 572430

e-mail:

THE INN AT WHITEWELL

Forest Of Bowland, Clitheroe, Lancashire BB7 3AT

Tel: 01200 448222 **Fax:** 01200 448298

e-mail:

ABBOTS OAK

Warren Hills Road, Near Coalville, Leicestershire LE67 4UY

Tel: 01530 832 328 **Fax:** 01530 832 328

e-mail:

THE OLD MANOR HOTEL

11-14 Sparrow Hill, Loughborough, Leicestershire LE11 1BT

Tel: 01509 211228 **Fax:** 01509 211128

e-mail: bookings@oldmanor.com

QUORN COUNTRY HOTEL

66 Leicester Road, Quorn, Leicestershire LE12 8BB

Tel: 01509 415050 **Fax:** 01509 415557

e-mail: reservations@quorncountryhotel.co.uk

STAPLEFORD PARK HOTEL, SPA, GOLF & SPORTING ESTATE

Nr Melton Mowbray, Leicestershire LE14 2EF

Tel: 01572 787 522 **Fax:** 01572 787 651

e-mail: reservations@stapleford.co.uk

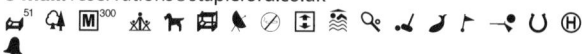

Sutton Bonington Hall

Main Street, Sutton Bonington, Loughborough, Leicestershire LE12 5PF

Tel: 01509 672355 **Fax:** 01509 674357

e-mail: enquiries@sutton-bonington-hall.com

Barnsdale Lodge

The Avenue, Rutland Water, Nr Oakham, Rutland, Leicestershire LE15 8AH

Tel: 01572 724678 **Fax:** 01572 724961

e-mail: barnsdale.lodge@btconnect.com

The Lea Gate Inn

Leagate Road, Coningsby, Lincolnshire LN4 4RS

Tel: 01526 342370 **Fax:** 01526 345468

e-mail: enquiries@theleagateinn.co.uk

Washingborough Hall

Church Hill, Washingborough, Lincoln LN4 1BE

Tel: 01522 790340 **Fax:** 01522 792936

e-mail: washingborough.hall@btinternet.com

The Olde Barn Hotel

Toll Bar Road, Marston, Lincolnshire NG32 2HT

Tel: 01400 250909 **Fax:** 01400 250130

e-mail: sales@oldebarnhotel.co.uk

The George Of Stamford

St Martins, Stamford, Lincolnshire PE9 2LB

Tel: 01780 750750 **Fax:** 01780 750701

e-mail: reservations@georgehotelofstamford.com

THE CROWN HOTEL

All Saints Place, Stamford, Lincolnshire PE9 2AG

Tel: 01780 763136 **Fax:** 01780 756111

e-mail: thecrownhotel@excite.com

LONDON - BELGRAVIA

THE HALKIN

5 Halkin Street, Belgravia, London SW1X 7DJ

Tel: 020 7333 1000 **Fax:** 020 7333 1100

e-mail: res@halkin.co.uk

LONDON - BLOOMSBURY

THE ACADEMY, THE BLOOMSBURY TOWN HOUSE

21 Gower Street, London WC1E 6HG

Tel: 020 7631 4115 **Fax:** 020 7636 3442

e-mail: res_academy@etontownhouse.com

LONDON - BUCKINGHAM PALACE

41

41 Buckingham Palace Road, London SW1W 0PS

Tel: 020 7300 0041 **Fax:** 020 7300 0141

e-mail: book41@rchmail.com

LONDON - BUCKINGHAM PALACE

THE RUBENS AT THE PALACE

39 Buckingham Palace Road, London SW1W 0PS

Tel: 020 7834 6600 **Fax:** 020 7828 5401

e-mail: bookrb@rchmail.com

LONDON - CANARY WHARF

CIRCUS APARTMENTS

39 Westferry Circus, Canary Wharf, London E14 8RW

Tel: 020 7719 7000 **Fax:** 020 7719 7001

e-mail: res@circusapartments.co.uk

Draycott House Apartments

10 Draycott Avenue, Chelsea, London SW3 3AA

Tel: 020 7584 4659   **Fax:** 020 7225 3694

e-mail: sales@draycotthouse.co.uk

Great Eastern Hotel

Liverpool Street, London EC2M 7QN

Tel: 020 7618 5000   **Fax:** 020 7618 5001

e-mail: sales@great-eastern-hotel.co.uk

London Bridge Hotel & Apartments

8–18 London Bridge Street, London SE1 9SG

Tel: 020 7855 2200   **Fax:** 020 7855 2233

e-mail: sales@london–bridge–hotel.co.uk

Kingsway Hall

Great Queen Street, London WC2B 5BX

Tel: 020 7309 0909   **Fax:** 020 7309 9696

e-mail: kingswayhall@compuserve.com

One Aldwych

1 Aldwych, London WC2B 4RH

Tel: 020 7300 1000   **Fax:** 020 7300 1001

e-mail: reservations@onealdwych.com

Oak Lodge Hotel

80 Village Road, Bush Hill Park, Enfield, Middlesex EN1 2EU

Tel: 020 8360 7082

e-mail: oaklodge@f.smail.net

West Lodge Park Country House Hotel

Cockfosters Road, Hadley Wood, Barnet, Hertfordshire EN4 0PY

Tel: 020 8216 3900 **Fax:** 020 8216 3937

e-mail: info@westlodgepark.com

Harrington Hall

5-25 Harrington Gardens, London SW7 4JW

Tel: 020 7396 9696 **Fax:** 020 7396 9090

e-mail: harringtonsales@compuserve.com

Kensington House Hotel

15-16 Prince Of Wales Terrace, Kensington, London W8 5PQ

Tel: 020 7937 2345 **Fax:** 020 7368 6700

e-mail: reservations@kenhouse.com

The Lexham Apartments

32-38 Lexham Gardens, Kensington, London W8 5JE

Tel: 020 7559 4444 **Fax:** 020 7559 4400

e-mail: reservations@lexham.com

The Milestone Hotel & Apartments

1 Kensington Court, London W8 5DL

Tel: 020 7917 1000 **Fax:** 020 7917 1010

e-mail: bookms@rchmail.com

Twenty Nevern Square

London SW5 9PD

Tel: 020 7565 9555 **Fax:** 020 7565 9444

e-mail: hotel@twentynevernsquare.co.uk

WARREN HOUSE

Warren Road, Coombe, Kingston-upon-thames, Surrey KT2 7HY

Tel: 020 8547 1777 **Fax:** 020 8547 1175

e-mail: carolyn@warrenhouse.com

BASIL STREET HOTEL

Basil Street, London SW3 1AH

Tel: 020 7581 3311 **Fax:** 020 7581 3693

e-mail: info@thebasil.com

BEAUFORT HOUSE

45 Beaufort Gardens, Knightsbridge, London SW3 1PN

Tel: 020 7584 2600 **Fax:** 020 7584 6532

e-mail: info@beauforthouse.co.uk

NUMBER ELEVEN CADOGAN GARDENS

11 Cadogan Gardens, Sloane Square, Knightsbridge, London SW3 2RJ

Tel: 020 7730 7000 **Fax:** 020 7730 5217

e-mail: reservations@number–eleven.co.uk

THE BEAUFORT

33 Beaufort Gardens, Knightsbridge, London SW3 1PP

Tel: 020 7584 5252 **Fax:** 020 7589 2834

e-mail: enquiries@thebeaufort.co.uk

THE CADOGAN

Sloane Street, London SW1X 9SG

Tel: 020 7235 7141 **Fax:** 020 7245 0994

e-mail: info@cadogan.com

THE CAPITAL HOTEL & APARTMENTS

22-24 Basil Street, Knightsbridge, London SW3 1AT

Tel: 020 7589 5171 **Fax:** 020 7225 0011

e-mail: reservations@capitalhotel.co.uk

THE CLIVEDEN TOWN HOUSE

26 Cadogan Gardens, London SW3 2RP

Tel: 020 7730 6466 **Fax:** 020 7730 0236

e-mail: reservations@clivedentownhouse.co.uk

THE COLONNADE, THE LITTLE VENICE TOWN HOUSE

2 Warrington Crescent, London W9 1ER

Tel: 020 7286 1052 **Fax:** 020 7286 1057

e-mail: res_colonnade@etontownhouse.com

THE LEONARD

15 Seymour Street, London W1H 7JW

Tel: 020 7935 2010 **Fax:** 020 7935 67000

e-mail: the.leonard@dial.pipex.com

DORSET SQUARE HOTEL

39 Dorset Square, Marylebone, London NW1 6QN

Tel: 020 7723 7874 **Fax:** 020 7724 3328

e-mail: dorset@firmdale.com

THE ASCOTT MAYFAIR

49 Hill Street, London W1J 5NB

Tel: 020 7659 4321 **Fax:** 020 7659 4322

e-mail: enquiry.london@the–ascott.com

THE CHESTERFIELD MAYFAIR

35 Charles Street, Mayfair, London W1J 5EB

Tel: 020 7491 2622 **Fax:** 020 7491 4793

e-mail: book@rchmail.com

THE DORCHESTER

Park Lane, Mayfair, London W1A 2HJ

Tel: 020 7629 8888 **Fax:** 020 7409 0114

e-mail: reservations@dorchesterhotel.com

THE WESTBOURNE

165 Westbourne Grove, Notting Hill, London W11 2RS

Tel: 020 7243 6008 **Fax:** 020 7229 7201

e-mail: info@aliaswestbourne.com

PEMBRIDGE COURT HOTEL

34 Pembridge Gardens, London W2 4DX

Tel: 020 7229 9977 **Fax:** 020 7727 4982

e-mail: reservations@pemct.co.uk

THE ATHENAEUM HOTEL & APARTMENTS

116 Piccadilly, London W1J 7BJ

Tel: 020 7499 3464 **Fax:** 020 7493 1860

e-mail: info@athenaeumhotel.com

THE PETERSHAM

Nightingale Lane, Richmond-upon-thames, Surrey TW10 6UZ

Tel: 020 8940 7471 **Fax:** 020 8939 1098

e-mail: enq@petershamhotel.co.uk

The Richmond Gate Hotel And Restaurant

Richmond Hill, Richmond-upon-thames, Surrey TW10 6RP

Tel: 020 8940 0061 **Fax:** 020 8332 0354

e-mail: richmondgate@corushotels.com

Number Sixteen

16 Sumner Place, London SW7 3EG

Tel: 020 7589 5232 **Fax:** 020 7584 8615

e-mail: reservations@numbersixteenhotel.co.uk

The Cranley

10-12 Bina Gardens, South Kensington, London SW5 0LA

Tel: 020 7373 0123 **Fax:** 020 7373 9497

e-mail: info@thecranley.com

The Gallery

8-10, Queensberry Place, South Kensington, London SW7 2EA

Tel: 020 7915 0000 **Fax:** 020 7915 4400

e-mail: reservations@eeh.co.uk

The Pelham Hotel

15 Cromwell Place, London SW7 2LA

Tel: 020 7589 8288 **Fax:** 020 7584 8444

e-mail: pelham@firmdale.com

The Queensgate

54 Queens Gate, London SW7 5JW

Tel: 020 7761 4000 **Fax:** 020 7761 4040

e-mail: enquiries@thequeensgate.com

DOLPHIN SQUARE HOTEL

Dolphin Square, Chichester Street, London SW1V 3LX

Tel: 020 7834 3800 **Fax:** 020 7798 8735

e-mail: reservations@dolphinsquarehotel.co.uk

51 BUCKINGHAM GATE

51 Buckingham Gate, Westminster, London SW1E 6AF

Tel: 020 7769 7766 **Fax:** 020 7828 5909

e-mail: info@51-buckinghamgate.co.uk

SPA

CANNIZARO HOUSE

West Side, Wimbledon Common, London SW19 4UE

Tel: 0870 333 9124 **Fax:** 020 8970 2753

e-mail: cannizarohouse@thistle.co.uk

ETROP GRANGE

Thorley Lane, Manchester Airport, Greater Manchester M90 4EG

Tel: 0161 499 0500 **Fax:** 0161 499 0790

e-mail: etropgrange@corushotels.com

DIDSBURY HOUSE

Didsbury Park, Didsbury Village, Manchester M20 5LT

Tel: 0161 448 2200 **Fax:** 0161 448 2525

e-mail: enquiries@didsburyhouse.co.uk

SPA

THE WHITE HART INN

51 Stockport Road, Lydgate, Saddleworth, Greater Manchester OL4 4JJ

Tel: 01457 872566 **Fax:** 01457 875190

e-mail: bookings@thewhitehart.co.uk

THE BERESFORD

1 Beresford Road, Oxton, Wirral CH43 1XQ
Tel: 0151 651 0004 **Fax:** 0151 652 4684
e-mail:

BARNHAM BROOM

Norwich, Norfolk NR9 4DD
Tel: 01603 759393 **Fax:** 01603 758224
e-mail: enquiry@barnhambroomhotel.co.uk

THE WHITE HORSE

Brancaster Staithe, Norfolk PE31 8BW
Tel: 01485 210262 **Fax:** 01485 210930
e-mail: reception@whitehorsebrancaster.co.uk

THE HOSTE ARMS HOTEL

The Green, Burnham Market, Norfolk PE31 8HD
Tel: 01328 738777 **Fax:** 01328 730103
e-mail: reception@hostearms.co.uk

VERE LODGE

South Raynham, Fakenham, Norfolk NR21 7HE
Tel: 01328 838261 **Fax:** 01328 838300
e-mail: major@verelodge.co.uk

THE MANOR HOUSE

Barsham Road, Great Snoring, Norfolk NR21 OHP
Tel: 01328 820597 **Fax:** 01328 820048
e-mail: gtsnoringmanorho@aol.com

Caldecott Hall

Fritton, Great Yarmouth, Norfolk NR31 9EY

Tel: 01493 488488 **Fax:** 01493 488553

e-mail: caldecotthall@supanet.com

J.D. Young

2-4 Market Place, Harleston, Norfolk IP20 9AD

Tel: 01379 852822 **Fax:** 01379 855370

e-mail: info@jdyoung.co.uk

The Victoria At Holkham

Park Road, Holkham, Wells-next-the-sea, Norfolk NR23 1RG

Tel: 01328 711008 **Fax:** 01328 711009

e-mail: victoria@holkham.co.uk

The Roman Camp Inn

Holt Road, Aylmerton, Norwich, Norfolk NR11 8QD

Tel: 01263 838291 **Fax:** 01263 837071

e-mail: romancamp@lineone.net

Felbrigg Lodge

Aylmerton, North Norfolk NR11 8RA

Tel: 01263 837588 **Fax:** 01263 838012

e-mail: info@felbrigglodge.co.uk

Petersfield House Hotel

Lower Street, Horning, Nr Norwich, Norfolk NR12 8PF

Tel: 01692 630741 **Fax:** 01692 630745

e-mail: reception@petersfieldhotel.co.uk

Congham Hall

Grimston, King's Lynn, Norfolk PE32 1AH

Tel: 01485 600250   **Fax:** 01485 601191

e-mail: reception@conghamhallhotel.co.uk

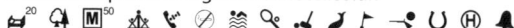

The Great Escape Holiday Company

Docking, Kings Lynn, Norfolk PE31 8LY

Tel: 01485 518717 **Fax:** 01485 518937

e-mail: bookings@thegreatescapeholiday.co.uk

Beechwood Hotel

Cromer Road, North Walsham, Norfolk NR28 0HD

Tel: 01692 403231 **Fax:** 01692 407284

e-mail: enquiries@beechwood-hotel.co.uk

Elderton Lodge Hotel & Langtry Restaurant

Gunton Park, Thorpe Market, Nr North Walsham, Norfolk NR11 8TZ

Tel: 01263 833547 **Fax:** 01263 834673

e-mail: enquiries@eldertonlodge.co.uk

The Beeches Hotel And Victorian Gardens

2–6 Earlham Road, Norwich, Norfolk NR2 3DB

Tel: 01603 621167 **Fax:** 01603 620151

e-mail: reception@beeches.co.uk

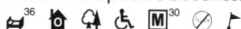

The Norfolk Mead Hotel

Coltishall, Norwich, Norfolk NR12 7DN

Tel: 01603 737531 **Fax:** 01603 737521

e-mail: info@norfolkmead.co.uk

THE STOWER GRANGE

School Road, Drayton, Norfolk NR8 6EF

Tel: 01603 860210 **Fax:** 01603 860464

e-mail: enquiries@stowergrange.co.uk

PARK FARM COUNTRY HOTEL & LEISURE

Hethersett, Norwich, Norfolk NR9 3DL

Tel: 01603 810264 **Fax:** 01603 812104

e-mail: enq@parkfarm–hotel.co.uk

THE OLD RECTORY

103 Yarmouth Road, Norwich, Norfolk NR7 OHF

Tel: 01603 700772 **Fax:** 01603 300772

e-mail: enquiries@oldrectorynorwich.com

BROVEY LAIR

Carbrooke Road, Ovington, Thetford, Norfolk IP25 6SD

Tel: 01953 882706 **Fax:** 01953 885365

e-mail: bookings@broveylair.co.uk

BROOM HALL COUNTRY HOTEL

Richmond Road, Saham Toney, Thetford, Norfolk IP25 7EX

Tel: 01953 882125 **Fax:** 01953 882125

e-mail: enquiries@broomhallhotel.co.uk

THE WINDMILL AT BADBY

Main Street, Badby, Daventry, Northamptonshire NN11 6AN

Tel: 01327 702363 **Fax:** 01327 311521

e-mail: user@windmillinn.fsnet.co.uk

NORTHAMPTONSHIRE - CASTLE ASHBY

THE FALCON HOTEL

Castle Ashby, Northamptonshire NN7 1LF

Tel: 01604 696200 **Fax:** 01604 696673

e-mail:

NORTHAMPTONSHIRE - DAVENTRY (FAWSLEY)

FAWSLEY HALL

Fawsley, Nr Daventry, Northamptonshire NN11 3BA

Tel: 01327 892000 **Fax:** 01327 892001

e-mail: reservations@fawsleyhall.com

NORTHAMPTONSHIRE - NORTHAMPTON (SILVERSTONE)

WHITTLEBURY HALL

Whittlebury, Nr Towcester, Northamptonshire NN12 8QH

Tel: 01327 857857 **Fax:** 01327 857867

e-mail: sales@whittleburyhall.co.uk

NORTHUMBERLAND - BAMBURGH

WAREN HOUSE HOTEL

Waren Mill, Bamburgh, Northumberland NE70 7EE

Tel: 01668 214581 **Fax:** 01668 214484

e-mail: enquiries@warenhousehotel.co.uk

NORTHUMBERLAND - BELFORD

THE BLUE BELL HOTEL

Market Place, Belford, Northumberland NE70 7NE

Tel: 01668 213543 **Fax:** 01668 213787

e-mail: bluebel@globalnet.co.uk

NORTHUMBERLAND - BERWICK-UPON-TWEED

MARSHALL MEADOWS COUNTRY HOUSE HOTEL

Berwick-upon-tweed, Northumberland TD15 1UT

Tel: 01289 331133 **Fax:** 01289 331438

e-mail: stay@marshallmeadows.co.uk

Tillmouth Park

Cornhill-on-tweed, Near Berwick-upon-tweed, Northumberland TD12 4UU

Tel: 01890 882255 **Fax:** 01890 882540

e-mail: reception@tillmouthpark.f9.co.uk

Matfen Hall

Matfen, Newcastle-upon-tyne, Northumberland NE20 0RH

Tel: 01661 886500 **Fax:** 01661 886055

e-mail: info@matfenhall.com

Linden Hall

Longhorsley, Morpeth, Northumberland NE65 8XF

Tel: 01670 50 00 00 **Fax:** 01670 50 00 01

e-mail: stay@lindenhall.co.uk

The Otterburn Tower

Otterburn, Northumberland NE19 1NS

Tel: 01830 520620 **Fax:** 01830 521504

e-mail: reservations@otterburntower.co.uk

Cockliffe Country House Hotel

Burnt Stump Country Park, Burnt Stump Hill, Nottinghamshire NG5 8PQ

Tel: 01159 680179 **Fax:** 01159 680623

e-mail: enquiries@cockliffehouse.co.uk

Hotel Des Clos

Old Lenton Lane, Nottingham, Nottinghamshire NG7 2SA

Tel: 01159 866566 **Fax:** 01159 860343

e-mail: info@hoteldesclos.com

Langar Hall

Langar, Nottinghamshire NG13 9HG

Tel: 01949 860559 **Fax:** 01949 861045

e-mail: langarhall–hotel@ndirect.co.uk

NOTTINGHAMSHIRE - NOTTINGHAM (RUDDINGTON)

The Cottage Country House Hotel

Easthorpe Street, Ruddington, Nottingham NG11 6LA

Tel: 01159 846882 **Fax:** 01159 214721

e-mail:

OXFORDSHIRE - BICESTER (CHESTERTON)

Bignell Park Hotel & Restaurant

Chesterton, Bicester, Oxfordshire OX26 1UE

Tel: 01869 362550 **Fax:** 01869 322729

e-mail: enq@bignellparkhotel.co.uk

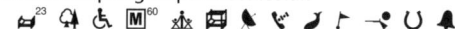

OXFORDSHIRE - BURFORD

The Bay Tree Hotel

Sheep Street, Burford, Oxon OX18 4LW

Tel: 01993 822791 **Fax:** 01993 823008

e-mail: bookings@cotswold–inns–hotels.co.uk

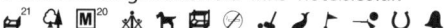

OXFORDSHIRE - BURFORD

The Lamb Inn

Sheep Street, Burford, Oxfordshire OX18 4LR

Tel: 01993 823155 **Fax:** 01993 822228

e-mail:

OXFORDSHIRE - CLANFIELD

The Plough At Clanfield

Bourton Road, Clanfield, Oxfordshire OX18 2RB

Tel: 01367 810222 **Fax:** 01367 810596

e-mail: ploughatclanfield@hotmail.com

The George Hotel

High Street, Dorchester-on-thames, Oxford OX10 7HH

Tel: 01865 340404 **Fax:** 01865 341620

e-mail:

OXFORDSHIRE - HENLEY-ON-THAMES

Phyllis Court Club

Marlow Road, Henley-on-thames, Oxfordshire RG9 2HT

Tel: 01491 570500 **Fax:** 01491 570528

e-mail: sue.gill@phylliscourt.co.uk

OXFORDSHIRE - OXFORD

The Cotswold Lodge Hotel

66a Banbury Road, Oxford OX2 6JP

Tel: 01865 512121 **Fax:** 01865 512490

e-mail: cotswoldlodgeuk@aol.com

OXFORDSHIRE - OXFORD (BANBURY)

Holcombe Hotel

High Street, Deddington, Nr Woodstock, Oxfordshire OX15 0SL

Tel: 01869 338274 **Fax:** 01869 337167

e-mail:

OXFORDSHIRE - OXFORD (BOARS HILL)

Westwood Country Hotel

Hinksey Hill, Nr. Boars Hill, Oxford OX1 5BG

Tel: 01865 735 408 **Fax:** 01865 736 536

e-mail: reservations@westwoodhotel.co.uk

OXFORDSHIRE - OXFORD (GREAT MILTON)

Le Manoir Aux Quat' Saisons

Great Milton, Oxfordshire OX44 7PD

Tel: 01844 278881 **Fax:** 01844 278847

e-mail: lemanoir@blanc.co.uk

STUDLEY PRIORY

Horton Hill, Horton-cum-studley, Oxford, Oxfordshire OX33 1AZ

Tel: 01865 351203 **Fax:** 01865 351613

e-mail: res@studley-priory.co.uk

FALLOWFIELDS

Kingston Bagpuize With Southmoor, Oxon OX13 5BH

Tel: 01865 820416 **Fax:** 01865 821275

e-mail: stay@fallowfields.com

THE JERSEY ARMS

Middleton Stoney, Oxfordshire OX25 4AD

Tel: 01869 343234 **Fax:** 01869 343565

e-mail: jerseyarms@bestwestern.co.uk

THE MILL & OLD SWAN

Minster Lovell, Nr. Burford, Oxfordshire OX29 5RN

Tel: 01993 774441 **Fax:** 01993 702002

e-mail: themill@initialstyle.co.uk

WESTON MANOR

Weston-on-the-green, Oxfordshire OX25 3QL

Tel: 01869 350621 **Fax:** 01869 350901

e-mail: reception@westonmanor.co.uk

THE SHAVEN CROWN HOTEL

High Street, Shipton Under Wychwood, Oxfordshire OX7 6BA

Tel: 01993 830330 **Fax:** 01993 832136

e-mail:

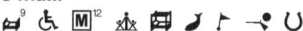

The Lamb Inn

Shipton-under-wychwood, Oxfordshire OX7 6DQ

Tel: 01993 830465 **Fax:** 01993 832025

e-mail: info@thelambinn.net

The Kings Head Inn & Restaurant

The Green, Bledington, Nr Kingham, Oxfordshire OX7 6XQ

Tel: 01608 658365 **Fax:** 01608 658902

e-mail: kingshead@orr-ewing.com

The Spread Eagle Hotel

Cornmarket, Thame, Oxfordshire OX9 2BW

Tel: 01844 213661 **Fax:** 01844 261380

e-mail: enquiries@spreadeaglethame.co.uk

The Springs Hotel & Golf Club

North Stoke, Wallingford, Oxfordshire OX10 6BE

Tel: 01491 836687 **Fax:** 01491 836877

e-mail: info@thespringshotel.com

The Feathers Hotel

Market Street, Woodstock, Oxfordshire OX20 1SX

Tel: 01993 812291 **Fax:** 01993 813158

e-mail: enquiries@feathers.co.uk

Hambleton Hall

Hambleton, Oakham, Rutland LE15 8TH

Tel: 01572 756991 **Fax:** 01572 724721

e-mail: hotel@hambletonhall.com

BARNSDALE LODGE

The Avenue, Rutland Water, Nr Oakham, Rutland LE15 8AH

Tel: 01572 724678 **Fax:** 01572 724961

e-mail: barnsdale.lodge@btconnect.com

RUTLAND - UPPINGHAM

THE LAKE ISLE

16 High Street East, Uppingham, Rutland LE15 9PZ

Tel: 01572 822951 **Fax:** 01572 824400

e-mail: Info@LakeIsleHotel.com

SHROPSHIRE - BRIDGNORTH (TELFORD)

THE OLD VICARAGE HOTEL

Worfield, Bridgnorth, Shropshire WV15 5JZ

Tel: 01746 716497 **Fax:** 01746 716552

e-mail: admin@the-old-vicarage.demon.co.uk

SHROPSHIRE - CHURCH STRETTON

STRETTON HALL

All Stretton, Church Stretton, Shropshire SY6 6HG

Tel: 01694 723224 **Fax:** 01694 724365

e-mail: enquiries@strettonhall.co.uk

SHROPSHIRE - LUDLOW

DINHAM HALL

Ludlow, Shropshire SY8 1EJ

Tel: 01584 876464 **Fax:** 01584 876019

e-mail: info@dinhamhall.co.uk

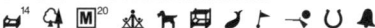

SHROPSHIRE - OSWESTRY

PEN-Y-DYFFRYN HALL HOTEL

Rhydycroesau, Nr Oswestry, Shropshire SY10 7JD

Tel: 01691 653700 **Fax:** 01691 650066

e-mail: stay@peny.co.uk

Prince Rupert Hotel

Butcher Row, Shrewsbury, Shropshire SY1 1UQ

Tel: 01743 499955 **Fax:** 01743 357306

e-mail: post@prince-rupert-hotel.co.uk

Madeley Court

Telford, Shropshire TF7 5DW

Tel: 01952 680068 **Fax:** 01952 684275

e-mail: admin@g6068.u–net.com

The Hundred House Hotel

Bridgnorth Road, Norton, Nr Shifnal, Telford, Shropshire TF11 9EE

Tel: 01952 730353 or 0845 130 0607 **Fax:** 01952 730355

e-mail: hundredhouse@lineone.net

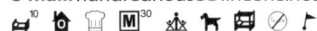

Soulton Hall

Nr Wem, Shropshire SY4 5RS

Tel: 01939 232786 **Fax:** 01939 234097

e-mail: j.ashton@soultonhall.fsbusiness.co.uk

Compton House

Townsend, Axbridge, Somerset BS26 2AJ

Tel: 01934 733944 **Fax:** 01934 733945

e-mail: info@comptonhse.com

Ston Easton Park

Ston Easton, Bath, Somerset BA3 4DF

Tel: 01761 241631 **Fax:** 01761 241377

e-mail: stoneastonpark@stoneaston.co.uk

WOOLVERTON HOUSE

Woolverton, Nr Bath, Somerset BA3 6QS

Tel: 01373 830415 **Fax:** 01373 831243

e-mail: mail@bathhotel.com

DANESWOOD HOUSE HOTEL

Cuck Hill, Shipham, Nr Winscombe, Somerset BS25 1RD

Tel: 01934 843145 **Fax:** 01934 843824

e-mail: info@daneswoodhotel.co.uk

ASHWICK COUNTRY HOUSE HOTEL

Dulverton, Somerset TA22 9QD

Tel: 01398 323868 **Fax:** 01398 323868

e-mail: ashwickhouse@talk21.com

THE CROWN HOTEL

Exford, Exmoor National Park, Somerset TA24 7PP

Tel: 01643 831554 **Fax:** 01643 831665

e-mail: info@crownhotelexmoor.co.uk

THE OLD RECTORY

Cricket Malherbie, Ilminster, Somerset TA19 0PW

Tel: 01460 54364 **Fax:** 01460 57374

e-mail: TheOldRectory@malherbie.freeserve.co.uk

ANDREW'S ON THE WEIR

Porlock Weir, Porlock, Somerset TA24 8PB

Tel: 01643 863300 **Fax:** 01643 863311

e-mail: information@andrewsontheweir.co.uk

Porlock Vale House

Porlock Weir, Somerset TA24 8NY

Tel: 01643 862338 **Fax:** 01643 863338

e-mail: info@porlockvale.co.uk

Charlton House And The Mulberry Restaurant

Charlton Road, Shepton Mallet, Near Bath, Somerset BA4 4PR

Tel: 01749 342008 **Fax:** 01749 346362

e-mail: enquiry@charltonhouse.com

Farthings Hotel & Restaurant

Hatch Beauchamp, Somerset TA3 6SG

Tel: 01823 480664 **Fax:** 01823 481118

e-mail: farthing1@aol.com

Mount Somerset Country House Hotel

Henlade, Taunton, Somerset TA3 5NB

Tel: 01823 442500 **Fax:** 01823 442900

e-mail: info@mountsomersethotel.co.uk

Bindon Country House Hotel

Langford Budville, Wellington, Somerset TA21 0RU

Tel: 01823 400070 **Fax:** 01823 400071

e-mail: stay@bindon.com

Langley House

Langley Marsh, Wiveliscombe, Somerset TA4 2UF

Tel: 01984 623318 **Fax:** 01984 624573

e-mail: info@langleyhousehotel.co.uk

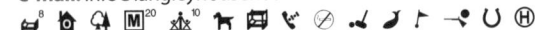

BERYL

Wells, Somerset BA5 3JP

Tel: 01749 678738 **Fax:** 01749 670508

e-mail: stay@beryl-wells.co.uk

GLENCOT HOUSE

Glencot Lane, Wookey Hole, Nr Wells, Somerset BA5 1BH

Tel: 01749 677160 **Fax:** 01749 670210

e-mail: relax@glencothouse.co.uk

THE SWAN HOTEL

Sadler Street, Wells, Somerset BA5 2RX

Tel: 01749 836300 **Fax:** 01749 836301

e-mail: swan@bhere.co.uk

THE WOODBOROUGH INN

Sandford Road, Winscombe, Somerset BS25 1HD

Tel: 01934 844167 **Fax:** 01934 843862

e-mail: info@woodborough-inn.co.uk

THE ROYAL OAK INN

Winsford, Exmoor National Park, Somerset TA24 7JE

Tel: 01643 851455 **Fax:** 01643 851009

e-mail: enquiries@royaloak–somerset.co.uk

CHESTNUT HOUSE

Hectors Stone, Lower Road, Woolavington, Bridgwater, Somerset TA7 8EQ

Tel: 01278 683658 **Fax:** 01278 684333

e-mail: jon@chestnuthouse.freeserve.co.uk

STAFFORDSHIRE - BIRMINGHAM NORTH (LICHFIELD)

SWINFEN HALL HOTEL

Swinfen, Nr Lichfield, Staffordshire WS14 9RE

Tel: 01543 481494 **Fax:** 01543 480341

e-mail: swinfenhall@virgin.net

STAFFORDSHIRE - BURTON UPON TRENT

YE OLDE DOG & PARTRIDGE

High Street, Tutbury, Burton-upon-trent, Staffordshire DE13 9LS

Tel: 01283 813030 **Fax:** 01283 813178

e-mail:

STAFFORDSHIRE - HOPWAS / LICHFIELD

OAK TREE FARM

Hints Road, Hopwas, Nr Tamworth, Staffordshire B78 3AA

Tel: 01827 56807 **Fax:** 01827 56807

e-mail:

STAFFORDSHIRE - LICHFIELD (HOAR CROSS)

HOAR CROSS HALL HEALTH SPA RESORT

Hoar Cross, Nr Yoxall, Staffordshire DE13 8QS

Tel: 01283 575671 **Fax:** 01283 575652

e-mail: info@hoarcross.co.uk

SUFFOLK - ALDEBURGH

WENTWORTH HOTEL

Wentworth Road, Aldeburgh, Suffolk IP15 5BD

Tel: 01728 452312 **Fax:** 01728 454343

e-mail: stay@wentworth–aldeburgh.co.uk

SUFFOLK - BURY ST EDMUNDS

ANGEL HOTEL

Bury St Edmunds, Suffolk IP33 1LT

Tel: 01284 714000 **Fax:** 01284 714001

e-mail: sales@angel.co.uk

RAVENWOOD HALL COUNTRY HOTEL & RESTAURANT

Rougham, Bury St Edmunds, Suffolk IP30 9JA

Tel: 01359 270345 **Fax:** 01359 270788

e-mail: enquiries@ravenwoodhall.co.uk

THE SUFFOLK GOLF & COUNTRY CLUB

Fornham St Genevieve, Bury St Edmunds, Suffolk IP28 6JQ

Tel: 01284 706777 **Fax:** 01284 706721

e-mail: thelodge@the-suffolk.co.uk

CLARICE HOUSE

Horringer Court, Horringer Road, Bury St. Edmunds Suffolk IP29 5PH

Tel: 01284 705550 **Fax:** 01284 716120

e-mail: enquire@clarice-bury.fsnet.co.uk

THE ICKWORTH HOTEL

Horringer, Bury St Edmunds, Suffolk IP29 5QE

Tel: 01284 735350 **Fax:** 01284 736300

e-mail: info@ickworthhotel.com

THE WHITE HORSE INN

Hollow Hill, Withersfield, Haverhill, Suffolk CB9 7SH

Tel: 01440 706081 **Fax:** 01440 706081

e-mail:

THE GEORGE

The Green, Cavendish, Sudbury, Suffolk CO10 8BA

Tel: 01787 280248 **Fax:** 01787 280248

e-mail: reservations@georgecavendish.co.uk

THE PLOUGH INN

Brockley Green, Nr Hundon, Sudbury, Suffolk CO10 8DT

Tel: 01440 786789 **Fax:** 01440 786710

e-mail:

THE MARLBOROUGH HOTEL

Henley Road, Ipswich, Suffolk IP1 3SP

Tel: 01473 226789/257677 **Fax:** 01473 226927

e-mail: sales@themarlborough.co.uk

BELSTEAD BROOK HOTEL

Belstead Road, Ipswich, Suffolk IP2 9HB

Tel: 01473 684241 **Fax:** 01473 681249

e-mail: sales@belsteadbrook.co.uk

HINTLESHAM HALL

Hintlesham, Ipswich, Suffolk IP8 3NS

Tel: 01473 652334 **Fax:** 01473 652463

e-mail: reservations@hintleshamhall.com

BLACK LION HOTEL & RESTAURANT

Church Walk, The Green, Long Melford, Suffolk CO10 9DN

Tel: 01787 312356 **Fax:** 01787 374557

BEDFORD LODGE HOTEL

Bury Road, Newmarket CB8 7BX

Tel: 01638 663175 **Fax:** 01638 667391

e-mail: info@bedfordlodgehotel.co.uk

Swynford Paddocks Hotel And Restaurant

Six Mile Bottom, Nr Newmarket, Suffolk CB8 0UE

Tel: 01638 570234 **Fax:** 01638 570283

e-mail: info@swynfordpaddocks.com

The Swan Hotel

Market Place, Southwold, Suffolk IP18 6EG

Tel: 01502 722186 **Fax:** 01502 724800

e-mail: swan.hotel@adnams.co.uk

Thornham Hall & Restaurant

Thornham Magna, Nr. Eye, Suffolk IP23 8HA

Tel: 01379 783314 **Fax:** 01379 788347

e-mail: lhenniker@thornhamhall.com

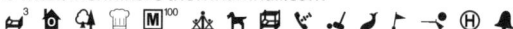

Seckford Hall

Woodbridge, Suffolk IP13 6NU

Tel: 01394 385678 **Fax:** 01394 380610

e-mail: reception@seckford.co.uk

Pennyhill Park Hotel

London Road, Bagshot, Surrey GU19 5EU

Tel: 01276 471774 **Fax:** 01276 473217

e-mail: enquiries@pennyhillpark.co.uk

Woodlands Park Hotel

Woodlands Lane, Stoke D'abernon, Cobham, Surrey KT11 3QB

Tel: 01372 843933 or 0800 9 177 877 **Fax:** 01372 842704

e-mail: info@woodlandspark.co.uk

SURREY - EGHAM

GREAT FOSTERS

Stroude Road, Egham, Surrey TW20 9UR

Tel: 01784 433822 **Fax:** 01784 472455

e-mail: enquiries@greatfosters.co.uk

SURREY - GATWICK (CHARLWOOD)

STANHILL COURT HOTEL

Stan Hill Road, Charlwood, Nr Horley, Surrey RH6 0EP

Tel: 01293 862166 **Fax:** 01293 862773

e-mail: enquiries@stanhillcourthotel.co.uk

SURREY - GATWICK (HORLEY)

LANGSHOTT MANOR

Langshott, Horley, Surrey RH6 9LN

Tel: 01293 786680 **Fax:** 01293 783905

e-mail: admin@langshottmanor.com

SURREY - GUILDFORD

THE ANGEL POSTING HOUSE AND LIVERY

91 The High Street, Guildford, Surrey GU1 3DP

Tel: 01483 564555 **Fax:** 01483 533770

e-mail: angelhotel@hotmail.com

SURREY - HAMPTON COURT (HAMPTON WICK)

CHASE LODGE

10 Park Road, Hampton Wick, Kingston-upon-thames, Surrey KT1 4AS

Tel: 020 8943 1862 **Fax:** 020 8943 9363

e-mail: info@chaselodgehotel.com

SURREY - HASLEMERE

LYTHE HILL HOTEL & SPA

Petworth Road, Haslemere, Surrey GU27 3BQ

Tel: 01428 651251 **Fax:** 01428 644131

e-mail: lythe@lythehill.co.uk

FOXHILLS

Stonehill Road, Ottershaw, Surrey KT16 0EL

Tel: 01932 704500 **Fax:** 01932 874762

e-mail: reservations@foxhills.co.uk

SURREY - REDHILL (NR GATWICK)

NUTFIELD PRIORY

Nutfield, Redhill, Surrey RH1 4EN

Tel: 01737 824400 **Fax:** 01737 823321

e-mail: nutbooking@aol.com

SURREY - WEYBRIDGE

OATLANDS PARK HOTEL

146 Oatlands Drive, Weybridge, Surrey KT13 9HB

Tel: 01932 847242 **Fax:** 01932 842252

e-mail: info@oatlandsparkhotel.com

EAST SUSSEX - ALFRISTON

WHITE LODGE COUNTRY HOUSE HOTEL

Sloe Lane, Alfriston, East Sussex BN26 5UR

Tel: 01323 870265 **Fax:** 01323 870284

e-mail: sales@whitelodge-hotel.com

EAST SUSSEX - BATTLE

POWDERMILLS HOTEL

Powdermill Lane, Battle, East Sussex TN33 0SP

Tel: 01424 775511 **Fax:** 01424 774540

e-mail: powdc@aol.com

EAST SUSSEX - BRIGHTON

THE GRANVILLE

124 Kings Road, Brighton BN1 2FA

Tel: 01273 326302 **Fax:** 01273 728294

e-mail: granville@brighton.co.uk

Buxted Park Country House Hotel

Buxted, Nr Uckfield, East Sussex TN22 4AY

Tel: 01825 732711 **Fax:** 01825 732770

e-mail: res.bph@arcadianhotels.co.uk

The Grand Hotel

King Edward's Parade, Eastbourne, East Sussex BN21 4EQ

Tel: 01323 412345 **Fax:** 01323 412233

e-mail: reservations@grandeastbourne.com

Ashdown Park Hotel And Country Club

Wych Cross, Forest Row, East Sussex RH18 5JR

Tel: 01342 824988 **Fax:** 01342 826206

e-mail: reservations@ashdownpark.com

Newick Park

Newick, Near Lewes, East Sussex BN8 4SB

Tel: 01825 723633 **Fax:** 01825 723969

e-mail: bookings@newickpark.co.uk

Horsted Place Country House Hotel

Little Horsted, East Sussex TN22 5TS

Tel: 01825 750581 **Fax:** 01825 750459

e-mail: hotel@horstedplace.co.uk

The Hope Anchor Hotel

Watchbell Street, Rye, East Sussex TN31 7HA

Tel: 01797 222216 **Fax:** 01797 223796

e-mail: info@hotel-rye.freeserve.co.uk

Dale Hill

Ticehurst, Nr Wadhurst, East Sussex TN5 7DQ

Tel: 01580 200112 **Fax:** 01580 201249

e-mail: info@dalehill.co.uk

Hooke Hall

High Street, Uckfield, East Sussex TN22 1EN

Tel: 01825 761578 **Fax:** 01825 768025

e-mail: a.percy@virgin.net

Amberley Castle

Amberley, Nr Arundel, West Sussex BN18 9ND

Tel: 01798 831992 **Fax:** 01798 831998

e-mail: info@amberleycastle.co.uk

Burpham Country House Hotel

Old Down, Burpham, Nr Arundel, West Sussex BN18 9RJ

Tel: 01903 882160 **Fax:** 01903 884627

e-mail: burphamchh@ukonline.co.uk

Bailiffscourt

Climping, West Sussex BN17 5RW

Tel: 01903 723511 **Fax:** 01903 723107

e-mail: bailiffscourt@hshotels.co.uk

The Mill House Hotel

Mill Lane, Ashington, West Sussex RH20 3BX

Tel: 01903 892426

e-mail: ashingtonmill@aol.com

Hotel Du Vin & Bistro

Ship Street, Brighton BN1 1AD

Tel: 01273 718588 **Fax:** 01273 718599

e-mail: info@hotelduvin.com

The Old Tollgate Restaurant And Hotel

The Street, Bramber, Steyning, West Sussex BN44 3WE

Tel: 01903 879494 **Fax:** 01903 813399

e-mail: otr@fastnet.co.uk

Crouchers Country Hotel & Restaurant

Birdham Road, Apuldram, Near Chichester, West Sussex PO20 7EH

Tel: 01243 784995 **Fax:** 01243 539797

e-mail:

The Millstream Hotel

Bosham, Nr Chichester, West Sussex PO18 8HL

Tel: 01243 573234 **Fax:** 01243 573459

e-mail: info@millstream–hotel.co.uk

Forge Hotel

Chilgrove, Chichester, West Sussex PO18 9HX

Tel: 01243 535333 **Fax:** 01243 535363

e-mail: reservations@forgehotel.com

Ockenden Manor

Ockenden Lane, Cuckfield, West Sussex RH17 5LD

Tel: 01444 416111 **Fax:** 01444 415549

e-mail: ockenden@hshotels.co.uk

....

Gravetye Manor

Near East Grinstead, West Sussex RH19 4LJ

Tel: 01342 810567 **Fax:** 01342 810080

e-mail: info@gravetyemanor.co.uk

WEST SUSSEX - GATWICK (TURNER'S HILL)
....

Alexander House Hotel

East Street, Turner's Hill, West Sussex RH10 4QD

Tel: 01342 714914 **Fax:** 01342 717328

e-mail: info@alexanderhouse.co.uk

WEST SUSSEX - HANDCROSS (SLAUGHAM)
....

The Chequers At Slaugham

Slaugham, Nr Handcross, West Sussex RH17 6AQ

Tel: 01444 400239/400996 **Fax:** 01444 400400

e-mail:

WEST SUSSEX - HORSHAM (NR GATWICK)
....

South Lodge Hotel

Lower Beeding, Nr Horsham, West Sussex RH13 6PS

Tel: 01403 891711 **Fax:** 01403 891766

e-mail: enquiries@southlodgehotel.co.uk

WEST SUSSEX - MIDHURST
....

The Angel Hotel

North Street, Midhurst, West Sussex GU29 9DN

Tel: 01730 812421 **Fax:** 01730 815928

e-mail: info@theangelmidhurst.co.uk

WEST SUSSEX - MIDHURST
....

The Spread Eagle Hotel & Health Spa

South Street, Midhurst, West Sussex GU29 9NH

Tel: 01730 816911 **Fax:** 01730 815668

e-mail: spreadeagle@hshotels.co.uk

THE HALF MOON INN

Kirdford, Near Petworth, West Sussex RH14 0LT

Tel: 01403 820223 **Fax:** 01403 820224

e-mail: halfmooninn.kirdford@virgin.net

HORTON GRANGE COUNTRY HOUSE HOTEL

Berwick Hill, Ponteland, Newcastle Upon Tyne NE13 6BU

Tel: 01661 860686 **Fax:** 01661 860308

e-mail: andrew@horton–grange.co.uk

THE VERMONT HOTEL

Castle Garth, Newcastle-upon-tyne, Tyne & Wear NE1 1RQ

Tel: 0191 233 1010 **Fax:** 0191 233 1234

e-mail: info@vermont-hotel.co.uk

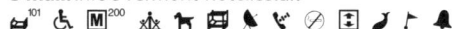

NAILCOTE HALL

Nailcote Lane, Berkswell, Nr Solihull, Warwickshire CV7 7DE

Tel: 02476 466174 **Fax:** 02476 470720

e-mail: info@nailcotehall.co.uk

NUTHURST GRANGE

Hockley Heath, Warwickshire B94 5NL

Tel: 01564 783972 **Fax:** 01564 783919

e-mail: info@nuthurst-grange.com

CLARENDON HOUSE

Old High Street, Kenilworth, Warwickshire CV8 1LZ

Tel: 01926 857668 **Fax:** 01926 850669

e-mail: info@clarendonhouse.com

Mallory Court

Harbury Lane, Bishops Tachbrook, Leamington Spa, Warwickshire
CV33 9QB

Tel: 01926 330214 **Fax:** 01926 451714

e-mail: reception@mallory.co.uk

Alveston Manor

Clopton Bridge, Stratford-upon-avon, Warwickshire CV37 7HP

Tel: 0870 400 8181 **Fax:** 01789 414095

e-mail: alvestonmanor@heritage-hotels.co.uk

Billesley Manor

Billesley, Alcester, Nr Stratford-upon-avon, Warwickshire B49 6NF

Tel: 01789 279955 **Fax:** 01789 764145

e-mail: bookings@billesleymanor.co.uk

Ettington Park

Alderminster, Stratford-upon-avon, Warwickshire CV37 8BU

Tel: 01789 450123   **Fax:** 01789 450472

e-mail: ettington@arcadianhotels.co.uk

The Welcombe Hotel And Golf Course

Warwick Road, Stratford-upon-avon, Warwickshire CV37 0NR

Tel: 01789 295252 **Fax:** 01789 414666

e-mail: sales@welcombe.co.uk

Glebe Farm House

Loxley, Warwickshire CV35 9JW

Tel: 01789 842501 **Fax:** 01789 842501

e-mail: scorpiolimited@msn.com

The Glebe At Barford

Church Street, Barford, Warwickshire CV35 8BS

Tel: 01926 624218 **Fax:** 01926 624625

e-mail: sales@glebe.co.uk

Ardencote Manor Hotel and Country Club

Lye Green Road, Claverdon, Warwickshire CV35 8LS

Tel: 01926 843111 **Fax:** 01926 842646

e-mail: hotel@ardencote.com

SPA

Wroxall Abbey Estate - Wroxall Court

Birmingham Road, Wroxall, Nr.warwick, Warwickshire CV35 7NB

Tel: 01926 484470 **Fax:** 01926 485206

e-mail: info@wroxallestate.com

Rudloe Hall

Leafly Lane, Near Box, Wiltshire SN13 0PA

Tel: 01225 810555 **Fax:** 01225 811412

e-mail: mail@rudloehall.co.uk

Widbrook Grange

Trowbridge Road, Bradford-on-avon, Nr Bath, Wiltshire BA15 1UH

Tel: 01225 864750/863173 **Fax:** 01225 862890

e-mail: stay@widbrookgrange.com

The Old Manor Hotel

Trowle, Bradford-on-avon, Wiltshire BA14 9BL

Tel: 01225 777393 **Fax:** 01225 765443

e-mail: romanticbeds@eastnet.co.uk

....

Lucknam Park, Bath

Colerne, Chippenham, Wiltshire SN14 8AZ

Tel: 01225 742777 **Fax:** 01225 743536

e-mail: reservations@lucknampark.co.uk

....

Hinton Grange

Nr. Hinton, Dryham, Wiltshire SN14 8HG

Tel: 0117 937 2916 **Fax:** 0117 937 3285

e-mail:

....

Woolley Grange

Woolley Green, Bradford-on-avon, Wiltshire BA15 1TX

Tel: 01225 864705 **Fax:** 01225 864059

e-mail: info@woolleygrange.com

....

The Manor House Hotel & Golf Club

Castle Combe, Chippenham, Wiltshire SN14 7HR

Tel: 01249 782206 **Fax:** 01249 782159

e-mail: enquiries@manor-housecc.co.uk

....

Stanton Manor

Stanton Saint Quintin, Nr Chippenham, Wiltshire SN14 6DQ

Tel: 01666 837552 **Fax:** 01666 837022

e-mail: reception@stantonmanor.co.uk

....

The Old Rectory

Crudwell, Nr Malmesbury, Wiltshire SN16 9EP

Tel: 01666 577194 **Fax:** 01666 577853

e-mail: office@oldrectorycrudwell.co.uk

WILTSHIRE - SALISBURY (TEFFONT EVIAS)

HOWARD'S HOUSE

Teffont Evias, Salisbury, Wiltshire SP3 5RJ

Tel: 01722 716392 **Fax:** 0722 716820

e-mail: enquiries@howardshousehotel.com

WILTSHIRE - SWINDON (PURTON)

THE PEAR TREE AT PURTON

Church End, Purton, Swindon, Wiltshire SN5 4ED

Tel: 01793 772100 **Fax:** 01793 772369

e-mail: relax@peartreepurton.co.uk

WILTSHIRE - WARMINSTER

BISHOPSTROW HOUSE

Warminster, Wiltshire BA12 9HH

Tel: 01985 212312 **Fax:** 01985 216769

e-mail: enquiries@bishopstrow.co.uk

WILTSHIRE - WARMINSTER (LONGBRIDGE DEVERILL)

THE GEORGE INN

Longbridge Deverill, Warminster, Wiltshire BA12 7DG

Tel: 01985 840396 **Fax:** 01985 841333

e-mail:

WORCESTERSHIRE - BROADWAY

DORMY HOUSE

Willersey Hill, Broadway, Worcestershire WR12 7LF

Tel: 01386 852711 **Fax:** 01386 858636

e-mail: reservations@dormyhouse.co.uk

WORCESTERSHIRE - BROADWAY

THE BROADWAY HOTEL

The Green, Broadway, Worcestershire WR12 7AA

Tel: 01386 852401 **Fax:** 01386 853879

e-mail: bookings@cotswold–inns–hotels.co.uk

BROCKENCOTE HALL

Chaddesley Corbett, Nr Kidderminster, Worcestershire DY10 4PY

Tel: 01562 777876 **Fax:** 01562 777872

e-mail: info@brockencotehall.com

THE EVESHAM HOTEL

Cooper's Lane, Off Waterside, Evesham, Worcestershire WR11 1DA

Tel: 01386 765566 **Fax:** 01386 765443

e-mail: reception@eveshamhotel.com

THE MILL AT HARVINGTON

Anchor Lane, Harvington, Evesham, Worcestershire WR11 8PA

Tel: 01386 870688 **Fax:** 01386 870688

e-mail: millatharvington@aol.com

THE MOUNT PLEASANT HOTEL

Belle Vue Terrace, Malvern, Worcestershire WR14 4PZ

Tel: 01684 561837 **Fax:** 01684 569968

e-mail: mountpleasanthotel@btinternet.com

COLWALL PARK

Colwall, Near Malvern, Worcestershire WR13 6QG

Tel: 01684 540000 **Fax:** 01684 540847

e-mail: hotel@colwall.com

THE COTTAGE IN THE WOOD

Holywell Road, Malvern Wells, Worcestershire WR14 4LG

Tel: 01684 575859 **Fax:** 01684 560662

e-mail: proprietor@cottageinthewood.co.uk

SALFORD HALL HOTEL

Abbots Salford, Nr Evesham, Worcestershire WR11 5UT

Tel: 01386 871300 **Fax:** 01386 871301

e-mail: reception@salfordhall.co.uk

THE WHITE LION HOTEL

High Street, Upton-upon-severn, Nr Malvern, Worcestershire WR8 0HJ

Tel: 01684 592551 **Fax:** 01684 593333

e-mail: reservations@whitelionhotel.demon.co.uk

WILLERBY MANOR HOTEL

Well Lane, Willerby, Hull, East Yorkshire HU10 6ER

Tel: 01482 652616 **Fax:** 01482 653901

e-mail: info@willerbymanor.co.uk

THE AUSTWICK COUNTRY HOUSE HOTEL & RESTAURANT

Austwick, Via Lancaster, North Yorkshire LA2 8BY

Tel: 015242 51224 **Fax:** 015242 51796

e-mail: austwick@aol.com

STOW HOUSE HOTEL

Aysgarth, Leyburn, North Yorkshire DL8 3SR

Tel: 01969 663635

e-mail: info@stowhouse.co.uk

THE DEVONSHIRE ARMS COUNTRY HOUSE HOTEL

Bolton Abbey, Skipton, North Yorkshire BD23 6AJ

Tel: reservations 01756 718111 **Fax:** 01756 710564

e-mail: sales@thedevonshirearms.co.uk

THE RED LION

By The Bridge At Burnsall, Near Skipton, North Yorkshire BD23 6BU

Tel: 01756 720204   **Fax:** 01756 720292

e-mail: redlion@daelnet.co.uk

CRATHORNE HALL

Crathorne, Nr Yarm, North Yorkshire TS15 0AR

Tel: 01642 700398   **Fax:** 01642 700814

e-mail: enquiries@crathornehall.com

THE BLUE LION

East Witton, Nr Leyburn, North Yorkshire DL8 4SN

Tel: 01969 624273   **Fax:** 01969 624189

e-mail: bluelion@breathemail.net

GRANTS HOTEL

Swan Road, Harrogate, North Yorkshire HG1 2SS

Tel: 01423 560666   **Fax:** 01423 502550

e-mail: enquiries@grantshotel–harrogate.com

RUDDING PARK HOTEL & GOLF

Rudding Park, Follifoot, Harrogate, North Yorkshire HG3 1JH

Tel: 01423 871350   **Fax:** 01423 872286

e-mail: sales@ruddingpark.com

THE BALMORAL HOTEL

Franklin Mount, Harrogate, North Yorkshire HG1 5EJ

Tel: 01423 508208   **Fax:** 01423 530652

e-mail: info@balmoralhotel.co.uk

Hob Green Hotel And Restaurant

Markington, Harrogate, North Yorkshire HG3 3PJ

Tel: 01423 770031 **Fax:** 01423 771589

e-mail: info@hobgreen.com

The Boar's Head Hotel

The Ripley Castle Estate, Harrogate, North Yorkshire HG3 3AY

Tel: 01423 771888 **Fax:** 01423 771509

e-mail: reservations@boarsheadripley.co.uk

Simonstone Hall

Hawes, North Yorkshire DL8 3LY

Tel: 01969 667255 **Fax:** 01969 667741

e-mail: email@simonstone.demon.co.uk

Rookhurst Country House Hotel

West End, Gayle, Hawes, North Yorkshire DL8 3RT

Tel: 01969 667454 **Fax:** 01969 667128

e-mail: rookhurst@lineone.net

The Pheasant

Harome, Helmsley, North Yorkshire YO62 5JG

Tel: 01439 771241 **Fax:** 01439 771744

e-mail:

Hazlewood Castle Hotel

Paradise Lane, Hazlewood, Tadcaster, Nr Leeds & York, North Yorkshire LS24 9NJ

Tel: 01937 535353 **Fax:** 01937 530630

e-mail: info@hazlewood-castle.co.uk

THE WHITE SWAN

The Market Place, Pickering, North Yorkshire YO18 7AA

Tel: 01751 472288 **Fax:** 01751 475554

e-mail: welcome@white-swan.co.uk

NORTH YORKSHIRE - RIPON (MASHAM)

SWINTON PARK

Masham, Nr Ripon, North Yorkshire HG4 4JH

Tel: 01765 680900 **Fax:** 01765 680901

e-mail: enquiries@swintonpark.com

NORTH YORKSHIRE - SCARBOROUGH (HACKNESS)

HACKNESS GRANGE

North York Moors National Park, Scarborough, North Yorkshire YO13 0JW

Tel: 01723 882345 **Fax:** 01723 882391

e-mail: hacknessgrange@englishrosehotels.co.uk

NORTH YORKSHIRE - SCARBOROUGH (SCALBY)

WREA HEAD COUNTRY HOTEL

Scalby, Nr Scarborough, North Yorkshire YO13 0PB

Tel: 01723 378211 **Fax:** 01723 355936

e-mail: wreahead@englishrosehotels.co.uk

NORTH YORKSHIRE - WHITBY

DUNSLEY HALL

Dunsley, Whitby, North Yorkshire YO21 3TL

Tel: 01947 893437 **Fax:** 01947 893505

e-mail:

NORTH YORKSHIRE - YORK

AMBASSADOR HOTEL

123–125 The Mount, York, North Yorkshire YO24 1DU

Tel: 01904 641316 **Fax:** 01904 640259

e-mail: stay@ambassadorhotel.co.uk

MIDDLETHORPE HALL

Bishopthorpe Road, York, North Yorkshire YO23 2GB

Tel: 01904 641241 **Fax:** 01904 620176

e-mail: info@middlethorpe.com

MOUNT ROYALE HOTEL

The Mount, York, North Yorkshire YO24 1GU

Tel: 01904 628856 **Fax:** 01904 611171

e-mail: reservations@mountroyale.co.uk

THE GRANGE HOTEL

1 Clifton, York, North Yorkshire YO30 6AA

Tel: 01904 644744 **Fax:** 01904 612453

e-mail: info@grangehotel.co.uk

THE WORSLEY ARMS HOTEL

Hovingham, Near York, North Yorkshire YO62 4LA

Tel: 01653 628234 **Fax:** 01653 628130

e-mail: worsleyarms@aol.com

MONK FRYSTON HALL HOTEL

Monk Fryston, North Yorkshire LS25 5DU

Tel: 01977 682369 **Fax:** 01977 683544

e-mail: reception@monkfryston-hotel.com

HELLABY HALL HOTEL

Old Hellaby Lane, Nr Rotherham, South Yorkshire S66 8SN

Tel: 01709 702701 **Fax:** 01709 700979

e-mail: sales@hellabyhallhotel.co.uk

CHARNWOOD HOTEL

10 Sharrow Lane, Sheffield, South Yorkshire S11 8AA

Tel: 0114 258 9411 **Fax:** 0114 255 5107

e-mail: reception@charnwoodhotel.co.uk

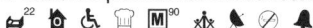

WHITLEY HALL HOTEL

Elliott Lane, Grenoside, Sheffield, South Yorkshire S35 8NR

Tel: 0114 245 4444 **Fax:** 0114 245 5414

e-mail: reservations@whitleyhall.com

HOLDSWORTH HOUSE

Holdsworth Road, Holmfield, Halifax, West Yorkshire HX2 9TG

Tel: 01422 240024 **Fax:** 01422 245174

e-mail: info@holdsworthhouse.co.uk

THE SHIBDEN MILL INN

Shibden Mill Fold, Shibden, Halifax, West Yorkshire HX3 7UL

Tel: 01422 365840 **Fax:** 01422 362971

e-mail: shibdenmillinn@zoom.co.uk

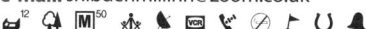

THE ROCK INN HOTEL

Holywell Green, Halifax, West Yorkshire HX4 9BS

Tel: 01422 379721 **Fax:** 01422 379110

e-mail: reservations@rockinnhotel.com

THE WEAVERS SHED RESTAURANT WITH ROOMS

Knowl Road, Golcar, Huddersfield, West Yorkshire HD7 4AN

Tel: 01484 654284 **Fax:** 01484 650980

e-mail: info@weaversshed.co.uk

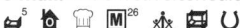

Haley's Hotel & Restaurant

Shire Oak Road, Headingley, Leeds, West Yorkshire LS6 2DE

Tel: 0113 278 4446 **Fax:** 0113 275 3342

e-mail: info@haleys.co.uk

Quebecs

9 Quebec Street, Leeds, West Yorkshire LS1 2HA

Tel: 0113 244 8989 **Fax:** 0113 244 9090

e-mail: res_quebecs@etontownhouse.com

Chevin Country Park Hotel

Yorkgate, Otley, West Yorkshire LS21 3NU

Tel: 01943 467818 **Fax:** 01943 850335

e-mail: reception@chevinlodge.co.uk

Wood Hall

Trip Lane, Linton, Nr Wetherby, West Yorkshire LS22 4JA

Tel: 01937 587271 or 0800 9 177 877 **Fax:** 01937 584353

e-mail: woodhall@arcadianhotels.co.uk

Channel Islands

La Favorita Hotel

Fermain Bay, Guernsey, Channel Islands GY4 6SD

Tel: 01481 235666 **Fax:** 01481 235413

e-mail: info@favorita.com

BELLA LUCE HOTEL & RESTAURANT

La Fosse, St Martins, Guernsey GY4 6EB

Tel: 01481 238764 **Fax:** 01481 239561

e-mail: info@bellalucehotel.guernsey.net

LES DOUVRES HOTEL & RESTAURANT

Rue De La Motte, St Martins, Guernsey GY4 6ER

Tel: 01481 238731 **Fax:** 01481 239683

e-mail: info@lesdouvreshotel.guernsey.net

LES ROCQUETTES HOTEL

Les Gravees, St Peter Port, Guernsey, Channel Islands GY1 1RN

Tel: 01481 722146 **Fax:** 01481 714543

e-mail: rocquettes@sarniahotels.com

THE WHITE HOUSE

Herm Island, Guernsey, Channel Islands GY1 3HR

Tel: 01481 722159 **Fax:** 01481 710066

e-mail: hotel@herm–island.com

CHÂTEAU LA CHAIRE

Rozel Bay, Jersey JE3 6AJ

Tel: 01534 863354 **Fax:** 01534 865137

e-mail: res@chateau-la-chaire.co.uk

HOTEL L'HORIZON

St Brelade's Bay, Jersey, Je3 8ef CHANNEL ISLANDS

Tel: 01534 743101 **Fax:** 01534 746269

e-mail: hotellhorizon@jerseymail.co.uk

THE ATLANTIC HOTEL

Le Mont De La Pulente, St Brelade, Jersey JE3 8HE

Tel: 01534 744101 **Fax:** 01534 744102

e-mail: info@theatlantichotel.com

EULAH COUNTRY HOUSE

Mont Cochon, St. Helier, Jersey JE2 3JA

Tel: 01534 626626 **Fax:** 01534 626600

e-mail: eulah@jerseymail.co.uk

LONGUEVILLE MANOR

St Saviour, Jersey JE2 7WF

Tel: 01534 725501 **Fax:** 01534 731613

e-mail: longman@itl.net

LA SABLONNERIE

Little Sark, Sark, Channel Islands GY9 0SD

Tel: 01481 832061 **Fax:** 01481 832408

e-mail:

Ireland

HYLAND'S BURREN HOTEL

Ballyvaughan, Co. Clare

Tel: 00 353 65 7077037 **Fax:** 00 353 65 7077131

e-mail: hylandsburren@eircom.net

Dromoland Castle

Newmarket-On-Fergus, Shannon Area, Co Clare

Tel: 00 353 61 368144   **Fax:** 00 353 61 363355

e-mail: sales@dromoland.ie

CORK - CORK CITY

Hayfield Manor Hotel

Perrott Avenue, College Road, Cork, Ireland

Tel: 00 353 21 4845900 **Fax:** 00 353 21 4316839

e-mail: enquiries@hayfieldmanor.ie

DONEGAL - DONEGAL TOWN

The Mill Park Hotel

Killybegs Road, Donegal Town, Co Donegal, Ireland

Tel: 00 353 73 22880 **Fax:** 00 353 73 22640

e-mail: millparkhotel@eircom.net

DUBLIN

Aberdeen Lodge

53 Park Avenue, Ballsbridge, Dublin 4, Ireland

Tel: 00 353 1 283 8155 **Fax:** 00 353 1 283 7877

e-mail: aberdeen@iol.ie

DUBLIN

Merrion Hall

54-56 MERRION ROAD, BALLSBRIDGE, DUBLIN 4

Tel: 00 353 1 668 1426 **Fax:** 00 353 1 668 4280

e-mail: merrionhall@iol.ie

DUBLIN

Stephen's Green Hotel

St Stephen'S Green, Dublin 2, Ireland

Tel: 00 353 1 607 3600 **Fax:** 0 353 1 661 5663

e-mail: stephensgreenres@ocallaghanhotels.ie

THE MERRION HOTEL

Upper Merrion Street, Dublin 2, Ireland

Tel: 00 353 1 603 0600 **Fax:** 00 353 1 603 0700

e-mail: info@merrionhotel.com

ROSS LAKE HOUSE HOTEL

Rosscahill, Oughterard, Co Galway, Ireland

Tel: 00 353 91 550109 **Fax:** 00 353 91 550184

e-mail: rosslake@iol.ie

CARAGH LODGE

Caragh Lake, Co Kerry

Tel: 00 353 66 9769115 **Fax:** 00 353 66 9769316

e-mail: caraghl@iol.ie

EMLAGH HOUSE

Dingle, Co Kerry, ireland

Tel: 00 353 66 915 2345 **Fax:** 00 353 66 915 2369

e-mail: info@emlaghhouse.com

GORMAN'S CLIFFTOP HOUSE & RESTAURANT

Glaise Bheag, Ballydavid, Dingle Peninsula – Tralee, Co Kerry

Tel: 00 353 66 9155162 **Fax:** 00 353 66 9155162

e-mail: gormans@eircom.net

SHEEN FALLS LODGE

Kenmare, Co. Kerry, Ireland

Tel: 00 353 64 41600 **Fax:** 00 353 64 41386

e-mail: info@sheenfallslodge.ie

SPA

KILLARNEY PARK HOTEL

Kenmare Place, Killarney, Co Kerry, Ireland

Tel: 00 353 64 35555 **Fax:** 00 353 64 35266

e-mail: info@killarneyparkhotel.ie

KILLARNEY ROYAL HOTEL

College Street, Killarney, Co Kerry, Ireland

Tel: 00 353 64 31853 **Fax:** 00 353 64 34001

e-mail: royalhot@iol.ie

PARKNASILLA HOTEL

Great Southern Hotel, Parknasilla, Co. Kerry, Ireland

Tel: 00 353 64 45122 **Fax:** 00 353 64 45323

e-mail: res@parknasilla.gsh.com

KILLASHEE HOUSE HOTEL

Killashee, Naas, Co Kildare, Ireland

Tel: 00 353 45 879277 **Fax:** 00 353 45 879266

e-mail: reservations@killasheehouse.com

MOUNT JULIET

Thomastown, Co. Kilkenny, Ireland

Tel: 00 353 56 73000 **Fax:** 00 353 56 73019

e-mail: info@mountjuliet.ie

ASHFORD CASTLE

Cong, Co Mayo

Tel: 00 353 92 46003 **Fax:** 00 353 92 46260

e-mail: ashford@ashford.ie

Knockranny House Hotel

Knockranny, Westport, Co Mayo, Ireland

Tel: 00 353 982 8600 **Fax:** 00 353 982 8611

e-mail: info@khh.ie

Nuremore Hotel And Country Club

Carrickmacross, Co Monaghan, Ireland

Tel: 00 353 42 9661438 **Fax:** 00 353 42 9661853

e-mail: nuremore@eircom.net

Coopershill House

Riverstown, Co Sligo

Tel: 00 353 71 65108 **Fax:** 00 353 71 65466

e-mail: ohara@coopershill.com

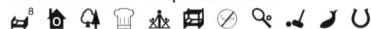

Cashel Palace Hotel

Main Street, Cashel, Co Tipperary

Tel: 00 353 62 62707 **Fax:** 00 353 62 61521

e-mail: reception@cashel–palace.ie

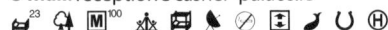

The Davenport Hotel

Merrion Square, Dublin 2, Ireland

Tel: 00 353 1 607 3500 **Fax:** 00 353 1 661 5663

e-mail: davenportres@ocallaghanhotels.ie

Dunbrody Country House & Restaurant

Arthurstown, New Ross, Co Wexford, Ireland

Tel: 00 353 51 389 600 **Fax:** 00 353 51 389 601

e-mail: dunbrody@indigo.ie

MARLFIELD HOUSE

Gorey, Co Wexford

Tel: 00 353 55 21124 **Fax:** 00 353 55 21572

e-mail: info@marlfieldhouse.ie

KILMOKEA COUNTRY MANOR & GARDENS

Kilmokea – Gt. Island, Campile, Co Wexford

Tel: 00 353 51 388109 **Fax:** 00 353 51 388776

e-mail: kilmokea@indigo.ie

KELLY'S RESORT HOTEL

Rosslare, Co Wexford, Ireland

Tel: 00 353 53 32114 **Fax:** 00 353 53 32222

e-mail: kellyhot@iol.ie

HUNTER'S HOTEL

Newrath Bridge, Rathnew, Co Wicklow

Tel: 00 353 404 40106 **Fax:** 00 353 404 40338

e-mail: reception@hunters.ie

Scotland

MARYCULTER HOUSE HOTEL

South Deeside Road, Maryculter, Aberdeen AB12 5GB

Tel: 01224 732124 **Fax:** 01224 733510

e-mail: info@maryculterhousehotel.com

Ardoe House Hotel And Restaurant

South Deeside Road, Blairs, Aberdeen AB12 5YP

Tel: 01224 860600 **Fax:** 01224 861283

e-mail: info@ardoe.macdonald-hotels.co.uk

Darroch Learg Hotel

Braemar Road, Ballater, Aberdeenshire AB35 5UX

Tel: 013397 55443 **Fax:** 013397 55252

e-mail: nigel@darrochlearg.co.uk

Balgonie Country House

Braemar Place, Ballater, Royal Deeside, Aberdeenshire AB35 5NQ

Tel: 013397 55482 **Fax:** 013397 55482

e-mail: balgoniech@aol.com

Castleton House Hotel

Glamis, By Forfar, Angus DD8 1SJ

Tel: 01307 840340 **Fax:** 01307 840506

e-mail: hotel@castletonglamis.co.uk

Ballachulish House

Ballachulish, Argyll PH49 4JX

Tel: 01855 811266 **Fax:** 01855 811498

e-mail: mclaughlins@btconnect.com

Kirkton House

Darleith Road, Cardross, Argyll & Bute G82 5EZ

Tel: 01389 841951 **Fax:** 01389 841868

e-mail: johan@kirktonhouse.co.uk

Enmore Hotel

Marine Parade, Kirn, Dunoon, Argyll PA23 8HH

Tel: 01369 702230 **Fax:** 01369 702148

e-mail: enmorehotel@btinternet.com

Isle of Eriska

Ledaig, By Oban, Argyll PA37 1SD

Tel: 01631 720371 **Fax:** 01631 720531

e-mail: office@eriska-hotel.co.uk

Ardanaiseig

Kilchrenan By Taynuilt, Argyll PA35 1HE

Tel: 01866 833333 **Fax:** 01866 833222

e-mail: ardanaiseig@clara.net

Barcaldine House

Barcaldine, Oban, Argyll PA37 1SG

Tel: 01631 720219 **Fax:** 01631 720219

e-mail: barcaldine@breathe.co.uk

Loch Melfort Hotel & Restaurant

Arduaine, By Oban, Argyll PA34 4XG

Tel: 01852 200233 **Fax:** 01852 200214

e-mail: reception@lochmelfort.co.uk

The Frog At Port Dunstaffnage

Dunstaffnage Marina, Connel, By Oban, Argyll PA37 1PX

Tel: 01631 567005 **Fax:** 01631 571044

e-mail: frogenqs@aol.com

STONEFIELD CASTLE

Tarbert, Loch Fyne, Argyll PA29 6YT

Tel: 01880 820836 **Fax:** 01880 820929

e-mail: enquiries@stonefieldcastle.co.uk

ROYAL HOTEL

Tighnabruaich, Argyll, Scotland PA21 2BE

Tel: 01700 811239 **Fax:** 01700 811300

e-mail: info@royalhotel.org.uk

WESTERN ISLES HOTEL

Tobermory, Isle Of Mull, Argyllshire PA75 6PR

Tel: 01688 302012 **Fax:** 01688 302297

e-mail: wihotel@aol.com

BALCARY BAY HOTEL

Auchencairn, Nr Castle Douglas, Dumfries & Galloway DG7 1QZ

Tel: 01556 640217/640311 **Fax:** 01556 640272

e-mail: reservations@balcary-bay-hotel.co.uk

CALLY PALACE HOTEL

Gatehouse Of Fleet, Dumfries & Galloway DG7 2DL

Tel: 01557 814341 **Fax:** 01557 814522

e-mail: info@callypalace.co.uk

KIRROUGHTREE HOUSE

Newton Stewart, Wigtownshire DG8 6AN

Tel: 01671 402141 **Fax:** 01671 402425

e-mail: info@kirroughtreehouse.co.uk

THE DRYFESDALE HOTEL

Lockerbie, Dumfriesshire DG11 2SF

Tel: 01576 202427 **Fax:** 01576 204187

e-mail: reception@dryfesdalehotel.co.uk

FERNHILL HOTEL

Heugh Road, Portpatrick DG9 8TD

Tel: 01776 810220 **Fax:** 01776 810596

e-mail: info@fernhillhotel.co.uk

THE BONHAM

35 Drumsheugh Gardens, Edinburgh EH3 7RN

Tel: 0131 623 6060 **Fax:** 0131 226 6080

e-mail: reserve@thebonham.com

BRUNTSFIELD HOTEL

69 Bruntsfield Place, Edinburgh EH10 4HH

Tel: 0131 229 1393 **Fax:** 0131 229 5634

e-mail: sales@thebruntsfield.co.uk

CHANNINGS

15 South Learmonth Gardens, Edinburgh EH4 1EZ

Tel: 0131 332 3232 **Fax:** 0131 332 9631

e-mail: reserve@channings.co.uk

THE HOWARD

34 Great King Street, Edinburgh EH3 6QH

Tel: 0131 315 2220 **Fax:** 0131 557 6515

e-mail: reserve@thehoward.com

PRESTONFIELD HOUSE

Priestfield Road, Edinburgh EH16 5UT

Tel: 0131 668 3346 **Fax:** 0131 668 3976

e-mail: info@prestonfieldhouse.com

THE ROXBURGHE

38 Charlotte Square, Edinburgh EH2 4HG

Tel: 0131 240 5500 **Fax:** 0131 240 5555

e-mail: roxburghe@csmm.co.uk

THE SCOTSMAN

20 North Bridge, Edinburgh EH1 1YT

Tel: 0131 556 5565 **Fax:** 0131 652 3652

e-mail: reservations@scotsmanhotel.com

THE RUSACKS

Plimour Links, St. Andrews, Fife KY16 9JQ

Tel: 01334 474321 **Fax:** 01334 477896

e-mail: general.rusacks@macdonald-hotels.co.uk

STRATHBLANE COUNTRY HOUSE HOTEL

Milngavie Road, Strathblane G63 9EH

Tel: 01360 770491 **Fax:** 01360 770345

e-mail: strathblane.info@countryhotels.net

CORRIEGOUR LODGE HOTEL

Loch Lochy, By Spean Bridge, Inverness-shire PH34 4EB

Tel: 01397 712685 **Fax:** 01397 712696

e-mail: info@corriegour-lodge-hotel.com

MUCKRACH LODGE HOTEL & RESTAURANT

Dulnain Bridge, By Grantown-on-spey, Inverness-shire PH26 3LY

Tel: 01479 851257 **Fax:** 01479 851325

e-mail: stay@muckrach.co.uk

BUNCHREW HOUSE HOTEL

Inverness, Scotland IV3 8TA

Tel: 01463 234917 **Fax:** 01463 710620

e-mail: welcome@bunchrew–inverness.co.uk

THE GLENMORISTON TOWN HOUSE HOTEL & LA RIVIERA RESTAURANT

Ness Bank, Inverness IV2 4SF

Tel: 01463 223777 **Fax:** 01463 712378

e-mail: glenmoriston@cali.co.uk

CULDUTHEL LODGE

14 Culduthel Road, Inverness, Inverness-shire IV2 4AG

Tel: 01463 240089 **Fax:** 01463 240089

e-mail: johansens@culduthel.com

HOTEL EILEAN IARMAIN

Sleat, Isle Of Skye IV43 8QR

Tel: 01471 833332 **Fax:** 01471 833275

e-mail: hotel@eilean–iarmain.co.uk

CUILLIN HILLS HOTEL

Portree, Isle Of Skye IV51 9QU

Tel: 01478 612003 **Fax:** 01478 613092

e-mail: office@cuillinhills.demon.co.uk

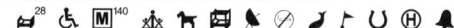

The Lodge On The Loch

Onich, Near Fort William, Highlands PH33 6RY

Tel: 01855 821237 **Fax:** 01855 821463

e-mail: reservations@freedomglen.co.uk

Glenmorangie House At Cadboll

Fearn, By Tain, Ross-shire IV20 1XP

Tel: 01862 871671 **Fax:** 01862 871625

e-mail: relax@glenmorangieplc.co.uk

Portland Arms Hotel

Lybster, Caithness KW3 6BS

Tel: 01593 721721 **Fax:** 01593 721722

e-mail: info@portlandarms.co.uk

Dalhousie Castle And Spa

Nr Edinburgh, Bonnyrigg EH19 3JB

Tel: 01875 820153

e-mail: enquiries@dalhousiecastle.co.uk

Borthwick Castle

Borthwick, North Middleton, Midlothian EH23 4QY

Tel: 01875 820514 **Fax:** 01875 821702

e-mail: borthwickcastle@hotmail.com

Knockomie Hotel

Grantown Road, Forres, Morayshire IV36 2SG

Tel: 01309 673146 **Fax:** 01309 673290

e-mail: stay@knockomie.co.uk

GLENEAGLES

Auchterarder, Perthshire PH3 1NF

Tel: 01764 662231 **Fax:** 01764 662134

e-mail: resort.sales@gleneagles.com

PERTH & KINROSS - BLAIRGOWRIE

KINLOCH HOUSE HOTEL

By Blairgowrie, Perthshire PH10 6SG

Tel: 01250 884237 **Fax:** 01250 884333

e-mail: reception@kinlochhouse.com

PERTH & KINROSS - COMRIE

THE ROYAL HOTEL

Melville Square, Comrie, Perthshire PH6 2DN

Tel: 01764 679200 **Fax:** 01764 679219

e-mail: reception@royalhotel.co.uk

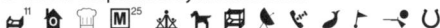

PERTH & KINROSS - DUNKELD

THE PEND

5 Brae Street, Dunkeld, Perthshire PH8 0BA

Tel: 01350 727586 **Fax:** 01350 727173

e-mail: molly@thepend.sol.co.uk

PERTH & KINROSS - GLENSHEE (BY BLAIRGOWRIE)

DALMUNZIE HOUSE

Spittal O'glenshee, Blairgowrie, Perthshire PH10 7QG

Tel: 01250 885224 **Fax:** 01250 885225

e-mail: dalmunzie@aol.com

PERTH & KINROSS - KILLIN

ARDEONAIG

South Loch Tay Side, By Killin, Perthshire FK21 8SU

Tel: 01567 820400 **Fax:** 01567 820282

e-mail: ardeonaighotel@btinternet.com

CROMLIX HOUSE

Kinbuck, By Dunblane, Nr Stirling FK15 9JT

Tel: 01786 822125 **Fax:** 01786 825450

e-mail: reservations@cromlixhouse.com

THE FOUR SEASONS HOTEL

St Fillans, Perthshire PH6 2NF

Tel: 01764 685333 **Fax:** 01764 685444

e-mail: info@thefourseasonshotel.co.uk

KINFAUNS CASTLE

Nr Perth, Perthshire PH2 7JZ

Tel: 01738 620777 **Fax:** 01738 620778

e-mail: email@kinfaunscastle.co.uk

PARKLANDS HOTEL & ACANTHUS RESTAURANT

St. Leonard's Bank, Perth PH2 8EB

Tel: 01738 622451 **Fax:** 01738 622046

e-mail: parklands.perth@virgin.net

BALLATHIE HOUSE HOTEL

Kinclaven, Stanley, Perthshire PH1 4QN

Tel: 01250 883268 **Fax:** 01250 883396

e-mail: email@ballathiehousehotel.com

KNOCKENDARROCH HOUSE

Higher Oakfield, Pitlochry, Perthshire PH16 5HT

Tel: 01796 473473 **Fax:** 01796 474068

e-mail: info@knockendarroch.co.uk

THE LAKE HOTEL

Port Of Menteith, Perthshire FK8 3RA

Tel: 01877 385258 **Fax:** 01877 385671

e-mail: enquiries@lake-of-menteith-hotel.com

BOWFIELD HOTEL & COUNTRY CLUB

Howwood, Renfrewshire PA9 1LA

Tel: 01505 705225 **Fax:** 01505 705230

e-mail: enquiries@bowfieldcountryclub.co.uk

GLEDDOCH HOUSE

Langbank, Renfrewshire PA14 6YE

Tel: 01475 540711 **Fax:** 01475 540201

EDNAM HOUSE HOTEL

Bridge Street, Kelso, Roxburghshire TD5 7HT

Tel: 01573 224168 **Fax:** 01573 226319

e-mail: contact@ednamhouse.com

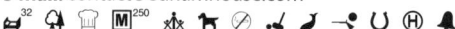

THE ROXBURGHE HOTEL & GOLF COURSE

Kelso, Roxburghshire TD5 8JZ

Tel: 01573 450331 **Fax:** 01573 450611

e-mail: hotel@roxburghe.net

CASTLE VENLAW

Edinburgh Road, Peebles EH45 8QG

Tel: 01721 720384 **Fax:** 01721 724066

e-mail: enquiries@evenlaw.co.uk

SOUTH AYRSHIRE - AYR

Enterkine House

Annbank, By Ayr, Ayrshire KA6 5AL

Tel: 01292 521608 **Fax:** 01292 521582

e-mail: mail@enterkine.com

SOUTH AYRSHIRE - AYR (SOUTH WEST SCOTLAND)

Culzean Castle – The Eisenhower Apartment

Maybole, Ayrshire KA19 8LE

Tel: 01655 884455 **Fax:** 01655 884503

e-mail: culzean@nts.org.uk

SOUTH AYRSHIRE - BALLANTRAE

Glenapp Castle

Ballantrae, Scotland KA26 0NZ

Tel: 01465 831212 **Fax:** 01465 831000

e-mail: enquiries@glenappcastle.com

SOUTH LANARKSHIRE - GLASGOW (EAST KILBRIDE)

Macdonald Crutherland House Hotel

Strathaven Road, East Kilbride G75 0QZ

Tel: 01355 577000 **Fax:** 01355 220855

e-mail: crutherland@macdonald–hotels.co.uk

STIRLING - ABERFOYLE (TROSSACHS)

Forest Hills Hotel

Kinlochard By Aberfoyle, The Trossachs FK8 3TL

Tel: 01877 387277 **Fax:** 01877 387307

e-mail: forest_hills@macdonald-hotels.co.uk

WEST LOTHIAN - EDINBURGH (INGLISTON)

The Norton House Hotel

Ingliston, Edinburgh EH28 8LX

Tel: 0131 333 1275 or 0800 9 177 877 **Fax:** 0131 333 5305

e-mail: nortonhouse@arcadianhotels.co.uk

Houstoun House

Uphall, Nr Edinburgh, Scotland EH52 6JS

Tel: 01506 853831 **Fax:** 01506 854220

e-mail: events.houstoun@macdonald-hotels.co.uk

Wales

ANGLESEY (TREARDDUR BAY)

The Trearddur Bay Hotel

Lon Isallt, Trearddur Bay, Anglesey LL65 2UN

Tel: 01407 860301   **Fax:** 01407 861181

e-mail: enquiries@trearddurbayhotel.co.uk

BRIDGEND - LALESTON

The Great House

High Street, Laleston, Bridgend, Wales CF32 0HP

Tel: 01656 657644 **Fax:** 01656 668892

e-mail: enquiries@great–house–laleston.co.uk

CARDIFF - ABERCYNON

Llechwen Hall

Abercynon, Nr Llanfabon, Cardiff, Mid Glamorgan CF37 4HP

Tel: 01443 742050 **Fax:** 01443 742189

e-mail: llechwen@aol.com

CARDIFF - ST BRIDES WENTLOOGE

Inn At The Elm Tree

St Brides Wentlooge, Nr Newport NP10 8SQ

Tel: 01633 680225 **Fax:** 01633 681035

e-mail: inn@the–elm–tree.co.uk

Conrah Country House Hotel

Rhydgaled, Chancery, Aberystwyth, Ceredigion SY23 4DF
Tel: 01970 617941 **Fax:** 01970 624546
e-mail: enquiries@conrah.co.uk

Ynyshir Hall

Eglwysfach, Machynlleth, Ceredigion SY20 8TA
Tel: 01654 781209 **Fax:** 01654 781366
e-mail: info@ynyshir-hall.co.uk

Sychnant Pass House

Sychnant Pass Road, Conwy LL32 8BJ
Tel: 01492 596868 **Fax:** 01492 596868
e-mail: bresykes@sychnant-pass-house.co.uk

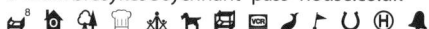

Tan-Y-Foel

Capel Garmon, Nr Betws-y-coed, Conwy LL26 0RE
Tel: 01690 710507 **Fax:** 01690 710681
e-mail: enquiries@tyfhotel.co.uk

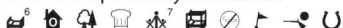

Castle Hotel

High Street, Conwy LL32 8DB
Tel: 01492 582 800 **Fax:** 01492 582 300
e-mail: mail@castlewales.co.uk

Bodysgallen Hall

Llandudno, North Wales LL30 1RS
Tel: 01492 584466 **Fax:** 01492 582519
e-mail: info@bodysgallen.com

St Tudno Hotel

North Promenade, Llandudno LL30 2LP

Tel: 01492 874411 **Fax:** 01492 860407

e-mail: sttudnohotel@btinternet.com

The Old Rectory Country House

Llanrwst Road, Llansanffraid Glan Conwy, Conwy LL28 5LF

Tel: 01492 580611 **Fax:** 01492 584555

e-mail: info@oldrectorycountryhouse.co.uk

The West Arms Hotel

Llanarmon D C, Ceiriog Valley, Nr Llangollen, Denbighshire LL20 7LD

Tel: 01691 600665 **Fax:** 01691 600622

e-mail: gowestarms@aol.com

Porth Tocyn Country House Hotel

Abersoch, Pwllheli, Gwynedd LL53 7BU

Tel: 01758 713303 **Fax:** 01758 713538

e-mail: porthtocyn.hotel@virgin.net

Bryn Tegid Country House

Bala, Gwynedd LL23 7YG

Tel: 01678 521645 **Fax:** 01678 521645

e-mail: info@bryntegid.co.uk

Palé Hall

Palé Estate, Llandderfel, Bala, Gwynedd LL23 7PS

Tel: 01678 530285 **Fax:** 01678 530220

e-mail: enquiries@palehall.co.uk

Bae Abermaw

Panorama Hill, Barmouth, Gwynedd LL42 1DQ

Tel: 01341 280550 **Fax:** 01341 280346

e-mail: bae.abermaw@virgin.net

Bontddu Hall

Bontddu, Nr Barmouth, Gwynedd LL40 2UF

Tel: 01341 430661 **Fax:** 01341 430284

e-mail: reservations@bontdduhall.co.uk

Plas Dolmelynllyn

Ganllwyd, Dolgellau, Gwynedd LL40 2HP

Tel: 01341 440273 **Fax:** 01341 440640

e-mail: info@dolly–hotel.co.uk

Penmaenuchaf Hall

Penmaenpool, Dolgellau, Gwynedd LL40 1YB

Tel: 01341 422129 **Fax:** 01341 422787

e-mail: relax@penhall.co.uk

Portmeirion And Castell Deudraeth

Portmeirion, Gwynedd LL48 6ET

Tel: 01766 770000 **Fax:** 01766 771331

e-mail: hotel@portmeirion–village.com

Ye Olde Bull's Head

Castle Street, Beaumaris, Isle Of Anglesey LL58 8AP

Tel: 01248 810329 **Fax:** 01248 811294

e-mail: info@bullsheadinn.co.uk

LLANSANTFFRAED COURT HOTEL

Llanvihangel Gobion, Abergavenny, Monmouthshire NP7 9BA

Tel: 01873 840678 **Fax:** 01873 840674

e-mail: reception@llch.co.uk

THE BELL AT SKENFRITH

Skenfrith, Monmouthshire NP7 8UH

Tel: 01600 750235 **Fax:** 01600 750525

e-mail: enquiries@thebellatskenfrith.com

PARVA FARMHOUSE AND RESTAURANT

Tintern, Chepstow, Monmouthshire NP16 6SQ

Tel: 01291 689411 **Fax:** 01291 689557

e-mail: Parva_hoteltintern@hotmail.com

STONE HALL HOTEL & RESTAURANT

Welsh Hook, Haverfordwest, Pembrokeshire SA62 5NS

Tel: 01348 840212 **Fax:** 01348 840815

e-mail: mstonehall@aol.co.uk

LAMPHEY COURT HOTEL

Lamphey, Nr Tenby, Pembrokeshire SA71 5NT

Tel: 01646 672273 **Fax:** 01646 672480

e-mail: info@lampheycourt.co.uk

WARPOOL COURT HOTEL

St David's, Pembrokeshire SA62 6BN

Tel: 01437 720300 **Fax:** 01437 720676

e-mail: warpool@enterprise.net

PENALLY ABBEY

Penally, Tenby, Pembrokeshire SA70 7PY

Tel: 01834 843033 **Fax:** 01834 844714

e-mail: penally.abbey@btinternet.com

POWYS - BRECON BEACONS (CWM TAF)

NANT DDU LODGE HOTEL

Cwm Taf, Brecon Beacons Nr Brecon, Powys, Wales CF48 2HY

Tel: 01685 379111 **Fax:** 01685 377088

e-mail: enquiries@nant–ddu–lodge.co.uk

POWYS - BRECON (LLANHAMLACH)

PETERSTONE COURT

Llanhamlach, Brecon, Powys LD3 7YB

Tel: 01874 665387   **Fax:** 01874 665376

e-mail: info@peterstone-court.com

POWYS - BRECON (LLYSWEN)

LLANGOED HALL

Llyswen, Brecon, Powys, Wales LD3 0YP

Tel: 01874 754525 **Fax:** 01874 754545

e-mail: Llangoed_Hall_Co_Wales_UK@compuserve.com

POWYS - CRICKHOWELL

GLIFFAES COUNTRY HOUSE HOTEL

Crickhowell, Powys NP8 1RH

Tel: 01874 730371 **Fax:** 01874 730463

e-mail: calls@gliffaeshotel.com

POWYS - CRICKHOWELL (ABERGAVENNY)

GLANGRWYNEY COURT

Glangrwyney, Nr Crickhowell, Powys NP8 1ES

Tel: 01873 811288 **Fax:** 01873 810317

e-mail: glangrwyney@aol.com

LAKE VYRNWY HOTEL

Lake Vyrnwy, Llanwddyn, Montgomeryshire SY10 0LY

Tel: 01691 870 692 **Fax:** 01691 870 259

e-mail: res@lakevyrnwy.com

THE LAKE COUNTRY HOUSE

Llangammarch Wells, Powys LD4 4BS

Tel: 01591 620202 **Fax:** 01591 620457

e-mail: info@lakecountryhouse.co.uk

MISKIN MANOR COUNTRY HOUSE HOTEL

Miskin, Nr Cardiff CF72 8ND

Tel: 01443 224204 **Fax:** 01443 237606

e-mail: info@miskin-manor.co.uk

NORTON HOUSE HOTEL AND RESTAURANT

Norton Road, Mumbles, Swansea SA3 5TQ

Tel: 01792 404891 **Fax:** 01792 403210

e-mail: nortonhouse@btconnect.com

EGERTON GREY

Porthkerry, Nr Cardiff, Vale OF GLAMORGAN

Tel: 01446 711666 **Fax:** 01446 711690

e-mail: info@egertongrey.co.uk

Europe & The Mediterranean

Andorra

ANDORRA (PAS DE LA CASA)

Font d'Argent Hotel Ski & Resort

C/ Bearn 20, 22, 24, Pas de La Casa, Andorra

Tel: +376 739 739 **Fax:** +376 739 800

e-mail: hotelfontdargent@hotelfontdargent.com

Austria

AUSTRIA / KÄRNTEN (KLAGENFURT)

Hotel Palais Porcia

Neuer Platz 13, 9020 Klagenfurt, Austria

Tel: +43 463 51 15 90 **Fax:** +43 463 51 15 90 30

e-mail: schlosshotel@mail.palais-porcia.co.at

AUSTRIA / KÄRNTEN (PATERGASSEN)

Almdorf "Seinerzeit"

Fellacheralm, 9564 Patergassen, Austria

Tel: +43 4275 7201 **Fax:** +43 4275 7201-6

e-mail: office@almdorf.com

SEESCHLÖSSL VELDEN

Klagenfurter Strasse 34, 9220 Velden, Austria

Tel: +43 4274 2824 **Fax:** +43 4274 2824 44

e-mail: seeschloessl@aon.at

HOTEL SCHLOSS DÜRNSTEIN

3601 Dürnstein, Austria

Tel: +43 2711 212 **Fax:** +43 2711 21230

e-mail: hotel@schloss.at

HOTEL & SPA HAUS HIRT

An Der Kaiserpromenade 14, 5640 Bad Gastein, Austria

Tel: +43 64 34 27 97 **Fax:** +43 64 34 27 97 48

e-mail: info@haus-hirt.com

DAS MOSER

Kaiser-Franz-Platz 2, 5630 Bad Hofgastein, Austria

Tel: + 43 6432 6209 **Fax:** +43 6432 6209 88

e-mail: info@gourmethotel–moser.com

GRAND PARK HOTEL BAD HOFGASTEIN

Kurgartenstrasse 26, 5630 Bad Hofgastein, Austria

Tel: +43 6432 63560 **Fax:** +43 6432 8454

e-mail: office@grandparkhotel.at

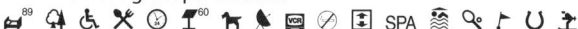

SCHLOSSHOTEL IGLS

Viller Steig 2, 6080 Igls, Tirol, Austria

Tel: +43 512 37 72 17 **Fax:** +43 512 37 72 17 198

e-mail: hotel@schlosshotel-igls.com

SPORTHOTEL IGLS

Hilberstrasse 17, 6080 Igls, Tirol, Austria

Tel: +43 512 37 72 41 **Fax:** +43 512 37 86 79

e-mail: hotel@sporthotel–igls.com

SPORTHOTEL KRISTIANIA

Omesberg 331, 6764 Lech Am Arlberg, Austria

Tel: +43 5583 25 610 **Fax:** +43 5583 3550

e-mail: kristiania@lech.at

THURNHERS ALPENHOF

6763 Zürs – Arlberg, Austria

Tel: +43 5583 2191 **Fax:** +43 5583 3330

e-mail: mail@thurnhers–alpenhof.at

GRAND HOTEL WIEN

Kärntner Ring 9, 1010 Vienna, Austria

Tel: +43 1 515 80 0 **Fax:** +43 1 515 13 13

e-mail: sales@grandhotelwien.com

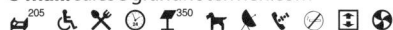

Belgium

FIREAN HOTEL

Karel Oomsstraat 6, 2018 Antwerp, Belgium

Tel: +32 3 237 02 60 **Fax:** +32 3 238 11 68

e-mail: info@hotel.fireancom

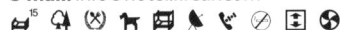

HOTEL ACACIA

Korte Zilverstraat 3A, 8000 Bruges, Belgium

Tel: +32 50 34 44 11 **Fax:** +32 50 33 88 17

e-mail: info@hotel-acacia.com

HOTEL DE TUILERIEËN

Dyver 7, 8000 Bruges, Belgium

Tel: +32 50 34 36 91 **Fax:** +32 50 34 04 00

e-mail: info@hoteltuilerieen.com

HOTEL MONTANUS

Nieuwe Gentweg 78, 8000 Bruges, Belgium

Tel: +32 50 33 11 76 **Fax:** +32 50 34 09 38

e-mail: info@montanus.be

HOTEL PRINSENHOF

Ontvangersstraat 9, 8000 Bruges, Belgium

Tel: +32 50 34 26 90 **Fax:** +32 50 34 23 21

e-mail: info@prinsenhof.be

ROMANTIK MANOIR CARPE DIEM

Prins Karellaan 12, 8420 de Haan, Belgium

Tel: +32 59 23 32 20 **Fax:** +32 59 23 33 96

e-mail: manoircarpediem@hotmail.com

HOSTELLERIE LE PRIEURÉ DE CONQUES

Rue de Conques 2, 6820 Florenville, Belgium

Tel: +32 61 41 14 17 **Fax:** +32 61 41 27 03

e-mail: info@conques.be

ROMANTIK HOTEL MANOIR DU DRAGON

Albertlaan 73, 8300 Knokke~Heist, Belgium

Tel: +32 50 63 05 80 **Fax:** +32 50 63 05 90

e-mail: manoirdudragon@pandora.be

HOTEL DAMIER

Grote Markt 41, 8500 Kortrijk, Belgium

Tel: +32 56 22 15 47 **Fax:** +32 56 22 86 31

e-mail: info@hoteldamier.be

HOSTELLERIE TRÔS MARETS

Route des Trôs Marets, 4960 Malmédy, Belgium

Tel: +32 80 33 79 17 **Fax:** +32 80 33 79 10

e-mail: tros.marets@skynet.be

CHÂTEAU D'HASSONVILLE

Route d'Hassonville 105, 6900 Marche~en~Famenne, Belgium

Tel: +32 84 31 10 25 **Fax:** +32 84 31 60 27

e-mail: info@hassonville.be

Cyprus

LE MERIDIEN LIMASSOL SPA & RESORT

Po Box 56560, 3308 Limassol, Cyprus

Tel: +357 25 862 000 **Fax:** +357 25 634 222

e-mail: enquiries@lemeridien~cyprus.com

Czech Republic

HOTEL HOFFMEISTER

Pod Bruskou 7, Klárov, 11800 Prague 1, Czech Republic

Tel: +420 2 51017 111 **Fax:** +420 2 51017 100

e-mail: hotel@hoffmeister.cz

ROMANTIK HOTEL U RAKA

Cerninska 10/93, 11800 Prague 1, Czech Republic.

Tel: +420 2205 111 00 **Fax:** +420 2333 580 41

e-mail: uraka@login.cz

SIEBER HOTEL & APARTMENTS

Slezská 55, 130 00 Prague 3, Czech Republic

Tel: +420 2 24 25 00 25 **Fax:** +420 2 24 25 00 27

e-mail: reservations@sieber.cz

Denmark

HOTEL HESSELET

Christianslundsvej 119, 5800 Nyborg, Denmark

Tel: +45 65 31 30 29 **Fax:** +45 65 31 29 58

e-mail: hotel@hesselet.dk

Estonia

VILLA AMMENDE

Mere Pst. 7, 80012 Pärnu, Estonia

Tel: +372 44 73888 **Fax:** +372 44 73887

e-mail: ammende@transcom.ee

France

FRANCE / ALSACE~LORRAINE (COLMAR)

HOSTELLERIE LE MARÉCHAL

4 Place Six Montagnes Noires, Petite Venise, 68000 Colmar, France

Tel: +33 3 89 41 60 32 **Fax:** +33 3 89 24 59 40

e-mail: marechal@calixo.net

FRANCE / ALSACE~LORRAINE (COLMAR)

HÔTEL LES TÊTES

19 Rue de Têtes, 68000 Colmar, France

Tel: +33 3 89 24 43 43 **Fax:** +33 3 89 24 58 34

FRANCE / ALSACE~LORRAINE (COLMAR - ROUFFACH)

CHÂTEAU D'ISENBOURG

68250 Rouffach, France

Tel: +33 3 89 78 58 50 **Fax:** +33 3 89 78 53 70

e-mail: contact@isenbourg.com

138

Hostellerie Les Bas Rupts

88400 Gérardmer, Vosges, France

Tel: +33 3 29 63 09 25 **Fax:** +33 3 29 63 00 40

e-mail: bas-rupts@wanadoo.fr

Hostellerie St Barnabé

68530 Murbach – Buhl, France

Tel: +33 3 89 62 14 14 **Fax:** +33 3 89 62 14 15

e-mail: hostellerie.st.barnabe@wanadoo.fr

A L'Ami Fritz

8 Rue des Châteaux, 67530 Ottrott, France

Tel: +33 3 88 95 80 81 **Fax:** +33 3 88 95 84 85

e-mail: hotel@amifritz.com

Château de L'Ile

4 Quai Heydt, 67540 Ostwald, France

Tel: +33 3 88 66 85 00 **Fax:** +33 3 88 66 85 49

e-mail: contact@chateau-ile.com

L'Horizon

50 Route du Crève~Cœur, 57100 Thionville, France

Tel: +33 3 82 88 53 65 **Fax:** +33 3 82 34 55 84

e-mail: hotel@lhorizon.fr

Hostellerie Château de Varillettes

15100 Saint~Georges par Saint~Flour, France

Tel: +33 4 71 60 45 05 **Fax:** +33 4 71 60 34 27

e-mail: varillettes@leshotelsparticuliers.com

DOMAINE DE ROCHEVILAINE

Pointe de Pen Lan, 56190 Billiers, France

Tel: +33 2 97 41 61 61 **Fax:** +33 2 97 41 44 85

CHÂTEAU DE BONABAN

35350 La Gouesnière, France

Tel: +33 2 99 58 24 50 **Fax:** +33 2 99 58 28 41

e-mail: chateau.bonaban@wanadoo.fr

DOMAINE DE LA BRETESCHE

44780 Missillac, France

Tel: +33 2 51 76 86 96 **Fax:** +33 2 40 66 99 47

e-mail: hotel@bretesche.com

MANOIR DE KERTALG

Route de Riec-Sur-Belon, 29350 Moelan~sur~Mer, France

Tel: +33 2 98 39 77 77 **Fax:** +33 2 98 39 72 07

CHÂTEAU DU LAUNAY

56160 Ploerdüt, France

Tel: +33 2 97 39 46 32 **Fax:** +33 2 97 39 46 31

LECOQ~GADBY

156 Rue d'Antrain, 35700 Rennes, France

Tel: +33 2 99 38 05 55 **Fax:** +33 2 99 38 53 40

e-mail: lecoq-gadby@wanadoo.fr

Manoir du Vaumadeuc

22130 Pleven, France

Tel: +33 2 96 84 46 17 **Fax:** +33 2 96 84 40 16

e-mail: manoir@vaumadeuc.com

Manoir de la Hazaie

22400 Planguenoual, France

Tel: +33 2 9632 7371 **Fax:** +33 2 9632 7972

e-mail: manoir.hazaie@wanadoo.fr

Ti Al Lannec

14 Allée de Mézo~Guen, BP 3, 22560 Trebeurden, France

Tel: +33 296 15 01 01 **Fax:** +33 2 96 23 62 14

e-mail: resa@tiallannec.com

Château de Vault de Lugny

11 Rue du Château, 89200 Avallon, France

Tel: +33 3 86 34 07 86 **Fax:** +33 3 86 34 16 36

e-mail: hotel@lugny.com

Hostellerie de la Poste

13 Place Vauban, 89200 Avallon, France

Tel: +33 3 86 34 16 16 **Fax:** +33 3 86 34 19 19

e-mail: info@hostelleriedelaposte.com

Ermitage de Corton

R.N. 74, 21200 Chorey~les~Beaune, France

Tel: +33 3 80 22 05 28 **Fax:** +33 3 80 24 64 51

HOSTELLERIE DES MONTS DE VAUX

Les Monts de Vaux, 39800 Poligny, France

Tel: +33 3 84 37 12 50 **Fax:** +33 3 84 37 09 07

e-mail: mtsvaux@hostellerie.com

LE PETIT MANOIR DES BRUYÈRES

5 Allée de Charbuy, les~Bruyères, 89240 Auxerre-Villefargeau, France

Tel: +33 3 86 41 32 82 **Fax:** +33 3 86 41 28 57

e-mail: jchambord@aol.com

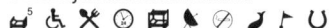

CHÂTEAU DE GILLY

Gilly~lès~Cîteaux, 21640 Vougeot, France

Tel: +33 3 80 62 89 98 **Fax:** +33 3 80 62 82 34

e-mail: gilly@grandesetapes.fr

HOSTELLERIE LA BRIQUETERIE

4 Route de Sézanne, 51530 Vinay – Épernay, France

Tel: +33 3 26 59 99 99 **Fax:** +33 3 26 59 92 10

e-mail: info@labriqueterie.com

L'ASSIETTE CHAMPENOISE

40 Avenue Paul Vaillant Couturier, 51430 Tinqueux, France

Tel: +33 3 26 84 64 64 **Fax:** +33 3 26 04 15 69

DOMAINE COCAGNE

Colline de La Route de Vence, 30, Chemin du Pain de Sucre, 08600 Cagnes~sur~Mer, France

Tel: +33 4 92 13 57 77 **Fax:** +33 4 92 13 57 89

e-mail: hotel@domainecocagne.com

Le Cavendish

11 Boulevard Carnot, 06400 Cannes, France

Tel: +33 4 97 06 26 00 **Fax:** +33 4 97 06 26 01

e-mail: reservation@cavendish-cannes.com

Château Eza

Rue De La Pise, 06360 Èze Village, France

Tel: +33 4 93 41 12 24 **Fax:** +33 4 93 41 16 64

e-mail: chateza@wanadoo.fr

Le Bailli de Suffren

Avenue des Américains, Golfe de Saint~Tropez, 83820 Le Rayol – Canadel, France

Tel: +33 4 98 04 47 00 **Fax:** +33 4 98 04 47 99

e-mail: info@lebaillidesuffren.com

Ermitage du Riou

Avenue Henri Clews, 06210 Mandelieu~La~Napoule, France

Tel: + 33 4 93 49 95 56 **Fax:** +33 4 92 97 69 05

e-mail: hotel@ermitage–du–riou.fr

Le Mas Candille

Boulevard Clément Rebuffel, 06250 Mougins, France

Tel: +33 4 92 28 43 43 **Fax:** +33 4 92 28 43 40

Hôtel La Pérouse

11, Quai Rauba~Capeu, 06300 Nice, France

Tel: +33 4 93 62 34 63 **Fax:** +33 4 93 62 59 41

e-mail: lp@hroy.com

LA FERME D'AUGUSTIN

Plage de Tahiti, 83350 Ramatuelle, Nr Saint-Tropez, France

Tel: +33 4 94 55 97 00 **Fax:** +33 4 94 97 40 30

e-mail: vallet.ferme.augustin@wanadoo.fr

LE MAS D'ARTIGNY

Route de la Colle, 06570 Saint~Paul~de~Vence, France

Tel: +33 4 93 32 84 54 **Fax:** +33 4 93 32 95 36

e-mail: mas@grandesetapes.fr

L'AUBERGE DU CHOUCAS

05220 Monetier~les~Bains, Serre~Chevalier, Hautes~Alpes, France

Tel: +33 4 92 24 42 73 **Fax:** +33 4 92 24 51 60

e-mail: auberge.du.choucas@wanadoo.fr

RELAIS CANTEMERLE

258 Chemin Cantemerle, 06140 Vence, France

Tel: +33 4 93 58 08 18 **Fax:** +33 4 93 58 32 89

e-mail: info@relais-cantemerle.com

CHÂTEAU DE PRAY

Route de Chargé, 37400 Amboise, France

Tel: +33 2 47 57 23 67 **Fax:** +33 2 47 57 32 50

e-mail: chateau.depray@wanadoo.fr

LE CHOISEUL

36 Quai Charles Guinot, 37400 Amboise, France

Tel: +33 2 47 30 45 45 **Fax:** +33 2 47 30 46 10

e-mail: choiseul@grandesetapes.fr

Le Manoir Les Minimes

34 Quai Charles Guinot, 37400 Amboise, France

Tel: +33 2 47 30 40 40 **Fax:** +33 2 47 30 40 77

e-mail: manoir-les-minimes@wanadoo.fr

Château de Danzay

RD 749, 37420 Chinon, France

Tel: +33 2 47 58 46 86 **Fax:** +33 2 47 58 84 35

e-mail: info@danzay.com

Hostellerie Château de Chissay

41400 Chissay~en~Touraine, France

Tel: +33 2 54 32 32 01 **Fax:** +33 2 54 32 43 80

e-mail: chissay@leshotelsparticuliers.com

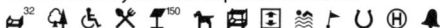

Château de Rochecotte

Saint~Patrice, 37130 Langeais, France

Tel: +33 2 47 96 16 16 **Fax:** +33 2 47 96 90 59

e-mail: chateau.rochecotte@wanadoo.fr

Le Prieuré

49350 Chênehutte~Les~Tuffeaux, France

Tel: +33 2 41 67 90 14 **Fax:** +33 2 41 67 92 24

e-mail: prieure@grandesetapes.fr

Domaine de Beauvois

Le Pont Clouet, Route de Clere~les~Pins, 37230 Luynes, France

Tel: +33 2 47 55 50 11 **Fax:** +33 2 47 55 59 62

e-mail: beauvois@grandesetapes.fr

CHÂTEAU D'ARTIGNY

37250 Montbazon, France

Tel: +33 2 47 34 30 30 **Fax:** +33 2 47 34 30 39

e-mail: artigny@grandesetapes.fr

DOMAINE DE LA TORTINIÈRE

Route de Ballan~Miré, 37250 Montbazon, France

Tel: +33 2 47 34 35 00 **Fax:** +33 2 47 65 95 70

e-mail: domaine.tortiniere@wanadoo.fr

LE GRAND ECUYER

Haut de la Cité, 81170 Cordes~Sur~Ciel, France

Tel: +33 5 63 53 79 50 **Fax:** +33 5 63 53 79 51

e-mail: grand.ecuyer@thuries.fr

BOIS JOLI

12, Avenue Philippe du Rozier, 61140 Bagnoles de L'Orne, France

Tel: +33 2 33 37 92 77 **Fax:** +33 2 33 37 07 56

e-mail: boisjoli@wanadoo.fr

CHÂTEAU DE GOVILLE

14330 Breuil~en~Bessin, France

Tel: +33 2 31 22 19 28 **Fax:** +33 2 31 22 68 74

e-mail: chateaugoville@wanadoo.fr

LE DONJON

Chemin de Saint Clair, 76790 Etretat, France

Tel: +33 2 35 27 08 23 **Fax:** +33 2 35 29 92 24

e-mail: info@ledonjon-etretat.fr

Manoir de la Poterie

Chemin Paul Ruel, 14113 Cricqueboeuf, France

Tel: +33 2 31 88 10 40 **Fax:** +33 2 31 88 10 90

e-mail: info@honfleur-hotel.com

Hostellerie Château de Brécourt

Douains, 27120 Pacy~sur~Eure, France

Tel: +33 2 32 52 40 50 **Fax:** +33 2 32 52 69 65

e-mail: brecourt@leshotelsparticulier.com

Abbatis Villa Hôtel Jean De Bruges

18, Place de L'Eglise, 80135 St. Riquier, France

Tel: +33 3 22 28 30 30 **Fax:** +33 3 22 28 00 69

e-mail: jeandebruges@wanadoo.fr

La Chartreuse du Val St Esprit

62199 Gosnay, France

Tel: +33 3 21 62 80 00 **Fax:** +33 3 21 62 42 50

e-mail: lachartreuse@gofornet.com

Château de Cocove

62890 Recques~sur~Hem, France

Tel: +33 3 21 82 68 29 **Fax:** +33 3 21 82 72 59

e-mail: chateaudecocove@hotmail.com

Château de Bellinglise

60157 Elincourt~Sainte~Marguerite, France

Tel: +33 3 44 96 00 33 **Fax:** +33 3 44 96 03 00

e-mail: chateaudebellinglise@wanadoo.fr

Hostellerie Château d'Ermenonville

60950 Ermenonville, France

Tel: +33 3 44 54 00 26 **Fax:** +33 3 44 54 01 00

e-mail: ermenonville@leshotelsparticuliers.com

Château de Fère

02130 Fère~en~Tardenois, France

Tel: + 33 3 23 82 21 13 **Fax:** +33 3 23 82 37 81

e-mail: chateau.fere@wanadoo.fr

Carlton Hotel

Rue de Paris, 59000 Lille, France

Tel: +33 3 20 13 33 13 **Fax:** +33 3 20 51 48 17

e-mail: carlton@carltonlille.com

La Tour du Roy

02140 Vervins, France

Tel: +33 3 23 98 00 11 **Fax:** +33 3 23 98 00 72

e-mail: latourduroy@wanadoo.fr

La Trémoille

14 Rue de La Trémoille, 75008 Paris, France

Tel: +33 1 56 52 14 00 **Fax:** +33 1 40 70 01 08

Hôtel Plaza Athénée

25 Avenue Montaigne, 75008 Paris, France

Tel: +33 1 53 67 66 65 **Fax:** +33 1 53 67 66 66

e-mail: reservation@plaza–athenee–paris.com

HÔTEL SAN REGIS

12 Rue Jean Goujon, 75008 Paris, France

Tel: +33 1 44 95 16 16 **Fax:** +33 1 45 61 05 48

e-mail: message@hotel-sanregis.fr

RÉSIDENCE ALMA MARCEAU****

5 Rue Jean Giraudoux, 75016 Paris, France

Tel: +33 1 53 57 67 89 **Fax:** +33 1 40 70 06 70

e-mail: infos@residencealmamarceau.com

L'HÔTEL PERGOLÈSE

3 Rue Pergolèse, 75116 Paris, France

Tel: +33 1 53 64 04 04 **Fax:** +33 1 53 64 04 40

e-mail: hotel@pergolese.com

LA VILLA MAILLOT

143 Avenue de Malakoff, 75116 Paris, France

Tel: +33 1 53 64 52 52 **Fax:** +33 1 45 00 60 61

e-mail: resa@lavillamaillot.fr

HÔTEL LE TOURVILLE

16 Avenue de Tourville, 75007 Paris, France

Tel: +33 1 47 05 62 62 **Fax:** +33 1 47 05 43 90

e-mail: hotel@tourville.com

LE SAINTE~BEUVE

9 Rue Sainte~Beuve, 75006 Paris, France

Tel: +33 1 45 48 20 07 **Fax:** +33 1 45 48 67 52

e-mail: saintebeuve@wanadoo.fr

HÔTEL DE L'ARCADE

9 Rue de L'Arcade, 75008 Paris, France

Tel: +33 1 53 30 60 00 **Fax:** +33 1 40 07 03 07

HÔTEL LE LAVOISIER

21 Rue Lavoisier, 75008 Paris, France

Tel: +33 1 53 30 06 06 **Fax:** +33 1 53 30 23 00

e-mail: info@hotellavoisier.com

HÔTEL LAMARTINE

39 Rue Lamartine, 75009 Paris, France

Tel: +33 1 48 78 78 58 **Fax:** +33 1 48 74 65 15

e-mail: lamartineopera@aol.com

HÔTEL DES GRANDS HOMMES

17 Place du Panthéon, 75005 Paris, France

Tel: +33 1 46 34 19 60 **Fax:** +33 1 43 26 67 32

e-mail: reservation@hoteldesgrandshommes.com

HÔTEL DU PANTHÉON

19 Place du Panthéon, 75005 Paris, France

Tel: +33 1 43 54 32 95 **Fax:** +33 1 43 26 64 65

e-mail: reservation@hoteldupantheon.com

ARTUSHOTEL

34 Rue de Buci, 75006 Paris, France

Tel: +33 1 43 29 07 20 **Fax:** +33 1 43 29 67 44

e-mail: info@artushotel.com

Hôtel Le Saint~Grégoire

43 Rue de L'Abbé Grégoire, 75006 Paris, France

Tel: 33 1 45 48 23 23 **Fax:** +33 1 45 48 33 95

e-mail: hotel@saintgregoire.com

Hôtel Pont Royal

7 Rue de Montalembert, 75007 Paris, France

Tel: +33 1 42 84 70 00 **Fax:** +33 1 42 84 71 00

e-mail: hpr@hotel-pont-royal.com

L' Hôtel

13, Rue des Beaux Arts, 75006 Paris, France

Tel: +33 1 44 41 99 00 **Fax:** +33 1 43 25 64 81

e-mail: reservation@l-hotel.com

Hostellerie Abbaye des Vaux de Cernay

78720 Cernay~La~Ville, France

Tel: +33 1 34 85 23 00 **Fax:** +33 1 34 85 11 60

e-mail: cernay@leshotelsparticuliers.com

Château d'Esclimont

28700 St. Symphorien~Le~Château, France

Tel: +33 2 37 31 15 15 **Fax:** +33 2 37 31 57 91

e-mail: esclimont@grandesetapes.fr

Le Manoir de Gressy

77410 Gressy~en~France, Roissy Cdg, Nr Paris, France

Tel: +33 1 60 26 68 00 **Fax:** +33 1 60 26 45 46

Les Étangs de Corot

53 Rue de Versailles, 92410 Ville d'Avray, France

Tel: +33 1 41 15 37 00 **Fax:** +33 1 41 15 37 99

e-mail: info@etangsdecorot.com

Hostellerie Château du Maréchal de Saxe

Domaine de La Grange, 91330 Yerres, France

Tel: +33 1 69 48 78 53 **Fax:** +33 1 69 83 84 91

e-mail: saxe@leshotelsparticuliers.com

Château de l'Yeuse

65 Rue de Bellevue, Quartier de Echassier, 16100 Châteaubernard, France

Tel: +33 5 45 36 82 60 **Fax:** +33 5 45 35 06 32

e-mail: yeuse@chateauxhotels.com

Manoir de Beauvoir Golf & Hôtel

635 Route de Beauvoir, 86550 Mignaloux – Beauvoir, France

Tel: +33 5 49 55 47 47 **Fax:** +33 5 49 55 31 95

e-mail: info@manoirdebeauvoir.com

Logis St. Martin

Chemin de Pissot, 79400 Saint~Maixent~L'Ecole, France

Tel: +33 549 0558 68 **Fax:** +33 549 7619 93

e-mail: courrier@logis-saint-martin.com

Le Pigonnet

5 Avenue du Pigonnet, 13090 Aix~en~Provence, France

Tel: +33 4 42 59 02 90 **Fax:** +33 4 42 59 47 77

e-mail: reservation@hotelpigonnet.com

Le Clair de la Plume

Place du Mail, 26230 Grignan, France

Tel: +33 4 75 91 81 30 **Fax:** +33 4 75 91 81 31

e-mail: plume2@wanadoo.fr

Manoir de la Roseraie

Route de Valréas, 26230 Grignan, France

Tel: +33 4 75 46 58 15 **Fax:** +33 4 75 46 91 55

e-mail: roseraie.hotel@wanadoo.fr

Mas de l'Oulivie

13520 Les~Baux~de~Provence, France

Tel: +33 4 90 54 35 78 **Fax:** +33 4 90 54 44 31

e-mail: contact@masdeloulivie.com

Mas de La Fouque

Route du Petit Rhône, 13460 Les Saintes~Maries~de~La~Mer, France

Tel: +33 4 90 97 81 02 **Fax:** +33 4 90 97 96 84

e-mail: fouque@wanadoo.fr

Château des Alpilles

Route Départementale 31, Ancienne Route du Grès, 13210
Saint~Rémy~de~Provence, France

Tel: +33 4 90 92 03 33 **Fax:** +33 4 90 92 45 17

e-mail: chateau.alpilles@wanadoo.fr

Château d'Arpaillargues

Hôtel Marie d'Agoult, 30700 Uzès, France

Tel: +33 4 66 22 14 48 **Fax:** +33 4 66 22 56 10

e-mail: SavryCHATEAU30@aol.com

CHÂTEAU DE LA TOUR DU PUITS

73800 Coise~Saint~Jean, France

Tel: +33 4 79 28 88 00 **Fax:** +33 4 79 28 88 01

e-mail: ctp@prevot.fr

HÔTEL ANNAPURNA

73120 Courchevel (1850), France

Tel: +33 4 79 08 04 60 **Fax:** +33 4 79 08 15 31

e-mail: info@annapurna-courchevel.com

LE KILIMANDJARO

Route de L'Altiport, 73121 Courchevel 1850 Cedex, France

Tel: +33 4 79 01 46 46 **Fax:** +33 4 79 01 46 40

e-mail: welcome@hotelkilimandjaro.com

CHÂTEAU DE DIVONNE

01220 Divonne~les~Bains, France

Tel: +33 4 50 20 00 32 **Fax:** +33 4 50 20 03 73

e-mail: divonne@grandesetapes.fr

LE DOMAINE DE DIVONNE CASINO, GOLF & SPA RESORT

Avenue des Thermes, 01220 Divonne-les-Bains, France

Tel: +33 4 50 40 34 34 **Fax:** +33 4 50 40 34 24

e-mail: info@domaine–de–divonne.com

CHALET HÔTEL LA MARMOTTE

61 Rue du Chéne, 74260 Les Gêts, France

Tel: + 33 4 50 75 80 33 **Fax:** +33 4 50 75 83 26

e-mail: info@hotel-marmotte.com

La Tour Rose

22 Rue du Boeuf, 69005 Lyon, France

Tel: +33 4 78 92 69 10 **Fax:** +33 4 78 42 26 02

e-mail: latourose@free.fr

Château de Coudrée

Domaine de Coudrée, Bonnatrait, 74140 Sciez~sur~Léman, France

Tel: +33 4 50 72 62 33 **Fax:** +33 4 50 72 57 28

e-mail: chcoudree@coudree.com

Hôtel du Palais

Avenue de L'Impératrice, 64200 Biarritz, France

Tel: +33 5 59 41 64 00 **Fax:** +33 5 59 41 67 99

e-mail: reception@hotel-du-palais.com

Le Manoir de Bellerive

Route de Siorac, 24480 Le-Buisson~de~Cadouin, France

Tel: +33 5 53 22 16 16 **Fax:** +33 5 53 22 09 05

e-mail: manoir.bellerive@wanadoo.fr

Hotel Lehen Tokia

Chemin Achotarreta, 64500 Ciboure, Saint~Jean~De~Luz, France

Tel: +33 5 59 47 18 16 **Fax:** +33 5 59 47 38 04

e-mail: info@lehen-tokia.com

Château de Sanse

33350 Sainte~Radegonde, France

Tel: +33 5 57 56 41 10 **Fax:** +33 5 57 56 41 29

e-mail: contact@chateaudesanse.com

CHÂTEAU DES BRIOTTIÈRES

49330 Champigné, France

Tel: +33 2 41 42 00 02 **Fax:** +33 2 41 42 01 55

e-mail: briottieres@wanadoo.fr

HOSTELLERIE ABBAYE DE VILLENEUVE

44480 Nantes – Les Sorinières, France

Tel: +33 2 40 04 40 25 **Fax:** +33 2 40 31 28 45

e-mail: villeneuve@leshotelsparticuliers.com

HOSTELLERIE DU GÉNÉRAL D'ELBÉE

Place du Château, 85330 Noirmoutier~en~L'Isle, France

Tel: +33 2 51 39 10 29 **Fax:** +33 2 51 33 08 23

e-mail: elbee@leshotelsparticuliers.com

Germany

HOTEL BURG WASSENBERG ****

Auf Dem Burgberg 1, 41849 Wassenberg, Germany

Tel: +49 2432 9490 **Fax:** +49 2432 949100

e-mail: burgwassenberg@t-online.de

BURGHOTEL AUF SCHÖNBURG

55430 Oberwesel – Rhein, Germany

Tel: +49 67 44 93 930 **Fax:** +49 67 44 16 13

e-mail: huettl@hotel–schoenburg.com

HOTEL EISENHUT

Herrngasse 3-7, 91541 Rothenburg Ob Der Tauber, Germany

Tel: +49 9861 7050 **Fax:** +49 9861 70545

e-mail: hotel@eisenhut.com

Greece

HOTEL PENTELIKON

66 Diligianni Street, 14562 Athens, Greece

Tel: +30 10 62 30 650-6 **Fax:** +30 10 80 19 223

e-mail: pentelik@otenet.gr

ST NICOLAS BAY HOTEL

72100 Agios Nikolaos, Crete, Greece

Tel: +30 2841 025041/2/3 **Fax:** +30 2841 024556

e-mail: stnicolas@otenet.gr

THE PENINSULA AT PORTO ELOUNDA DE LUXE RESORT

72053 Elounda, Crete, Greece

Tel: +30 28410 41903 **Fax:** +30 28410 41889

e-mail: porto@elounda-sa.com

ASTIR OF PAROS

Kolymbithres, Naoussa, 84401 Paro, Greece

Tel: +30 2840 51976 **Fax:** +30 2840 51985

e-mail: astir@hol.gr

Italy

HOTEL VILLA FRANCA

Viale Pasitea 318, 84017 Positano (SA), Italy

Tel: +39 089 875655 **Fax:** +39 089 875735

e-mail: hvf@starnet.it

HOTEL POSEIDON

Via Pasitea 148, 84017 Positano (Salerno), Italy

Tel: +39 089 811111 **Fax:** +39 089 875833

e-mail: info@hotelposeidonpositano.it

HOTEL VILLA MARIA

Via S.Chiara 2, 84010 Ravello (SA), Italy

Tel: +39 089 857255 **Fax:** +39 089 857071

OASI OLIMPIA RELAIS

Via Deserto 26, SanT'Agata sui due Golfi, 80064 Massa Lubrense (NA), Italy

Tel: +39 081 8080560 **Fax:** +39 081 8085214

e-mail: info@oasiolimpiarelais.it

GRAND HOTEL COCUMELLA

Via Cocumella 7, 80065 Sant'Agnello, Sorrento, Italy

Tel: +39 081 878 2933 **Fax:** +39 081 878 3712

e-mail: hcocum@tin.it

GRAND HOTEL EXCELSIOR VITTORIA

Piazza Tasso 34, 80067 Sorrento (Naples), Italy

Tel: +39 081 807 1044 **Fax:** +39 081 877 1206

e-mail: exvitt@exvitt.it

HOTEL TOSCO ROMAGNOLO

Piazza Dante Alighieri 2, 47021 Bagno di Romagna Terme, Italy

Tel: +39 0543 911260 **Fax:** +39 0543 911014

e-mail: lacasa@paoloteverini.it

GRAND HOTEL BAGLIONI

Via Indipendenza 8, 40121 Bologna, Italy

Tel: +39 051 225445 **Fax:** +39 051 234840

e-mail: ghb.bologna@baglionihotels.com

RELAIS TORRE PRATESI

Via Cavina 11, 48013 Brisighella, Italy

Tel: +39 0546 84545 **Fax:** +39 0546 84558

e-mail: torrep@tin.it

RIPAGRANDE HOTEL

Via Ripagrande 21, 44100 Ferrara, Italy

Tel: +39 0532 765250 **Fax:** +39 0532 764377

e-mail: ripahotel@mbox.4net.it

HOTEL DES NATIONS

Lungomare Costituzione 2, 47838 Riccione (Rn), Italy

Tel: +39 0541 647878 **Fax:** +39 0541 645154

e-mail: info@desnations.it

La Posta Vecchia

Loc. Palo Laziale, 00055 Ladispoli, Rome, Italy

Tel: +39 0699 49501 **Fax:** +39 0699 49507

e-mail: info@lapostavecchia.com

Hotel Aventino

Via San. Domenico 10, 00153 Rome, Italy

Tel: +39 06 5745 174 / 5783 214 **Fax:** +39 06 5783 604

e-mail: info@aventinohotels.com

Hotel Farnese

Via Alessandro Farnese 30 (Angolo Viale Giulio Cesare), 00192 Rome, Italy

Tel: +39 06 321 25 53/4 **Fax:** +39 06 321 51 29

Hotel Giulio Cesare

Via Degli Scipioni 287, 00192 Rome, Italy

Tel: +39 06 321 0751 **Fax:** +39 06 321 1736

e-mail: giulioce@uni.net

Hotel Punta Est

Via Aurelia 1, 17024 Finale Ligure, Italy

Tel: +39 019 600611 **Fax:** +39 019 600611/2

e-mail: info@puntaest.com

Hotel Vis à Vis & Ristorante Olimpo

Via della Chiusa 28, 16039 Sestri Levante, (GE), Italy

Tel: +39 0185 42661/480801 **Fax:** +39 0185 480853

e-mail: visavis@hotelvisavis.com

L'Albereta
Via Vittorio Emanuele 11, 25030 Erbusco (Bs), Italy

Tel: +39 030 7760 550 **Fax:** +39 030 7760 573

e-mail: info@albereta.it

Albergo San Lorenzo
Piazza Concordia 14, 46100 Mantova, Italy

Tel: +39 0376 220500 **Fax:** +39 0376 327194

e-mail: hotel@hotelsanlorenzo.it

Lovera Palace Hotel
Via Roma, 37, 12100 Cuneo, Italy

Tel: +39 0171 690 420 **Fax:** +39 0171 603 435

e-mail: info@loverapalace.com

Hotel Villa Aminta
Via Sempione Nord 123, 28838 Stresa (VB), Italy

Tel: +39 0323 933 818 **Fax:** +39 0323 933 955

e-mail: h.villaminta@stresa.net

Hotel Victoria
Via Nino Costa 4, 10123 Torino, Italy

Tel: +39 011 56 11909 **Fax:** +39 011 56 11806

e-mail: reservation@hotelvictoria–torino.com

Masseria San Domenico
Litoranea 379, 72010 Savelletri di Fasano (Brindisi) Italy

Tel: +39 080 482 7990 **Fax:** +39 080 482 7978

e-mail: info@masseriasandomenico.com

Hotel Villa Paradiso dell'Etna

Via Per Viagrande 37, 95037 San Giovanni La Punta, Italy

Tel: +39 095 7512409 **Fax:** +39 095 7413861

e-mail: hotelvilla@paradisoetna.it

Hellenia Yachting Hotel

Via Jannuzzo 41, 98035 Giardini Naxos (ME), Italy

Tel: +39 (0)942 51737 **Fax:** +39 (0)942 54310

e-mail: booking@hellenia-hotel.it

Hotel Baia Taormina

Statale Dello Ionio 39, 98030 Marina D'Agro (ME), Italy

Tel: +39 0942 756292 **Fax:** +39 0942 756603

e-mail: hotel@baiataormina.com

Hotel Lorenzetti

Via Dolomiti Di Brenta 119, 38084 Madonna Di Campiglio (Tn) Italy

Tel: +39 0465 44 14 04 **Fax:** +39 0465 44 06 88

e-mail: hotellorenzetti@hotellorenzetti.com

Romantik Hotel Oberwirt

St Felixweg 2, 39020 Marling – Meran, Italy

Tel: +39 0473 44 71 11 **Fax:** +39 0473 44 71 30

e-mail: info@oberwirt.com

Park Hotel Mignon

Via Grabmayr 5, 39012 Meran, Italy

Tel: +39 0473 230353 **Fax:** +39 0473 230644

e-mail: info@hotelmignon.com

POSTHOTEL WEISSES RÖSSL

Via Carezza 30, 39056 Nova Levante (Bz), Dolomites, Italy

Tel: +39 0471 613113 **Fax:** +39 0471 613390

e-mail: posthotel@postcavallino.com

HOTEL & SPA ROSA ALPINA

Strada Micura de Rue 20, 39030 San Cassiano (BZ) Italy.

Tel: +39 0471 849500 **Fax:** +39 0471 849377

e-mail: info@rosalpina.it

CASABIANCA

Loc. Casabianca , 53041 Asciano (SI), Italy

Tel: +39 0577 704362 **Fax:** +39 0577 704622

e-mail: casabianca@casabianca.it

RELAIS SAN PIETRO IN POLVANO

Località Polvano, 52043 Castiglion Fiorentino (AR), Italy

Tel: +39 0575 650100 **Fax:** +39 0575 650255

e-mail: polvano@technet.it

RELAIS DELLA ROVERE

Via Piemonte 10, Loc. Badia, 53034 Colle Val D'Elsa (SI), Italy

Tel: +39 0577 924696 **Fax:** +39 0577 924489

e-mail: dellarovere@chiantiturismo.it

GRAND HOTEL ELBA INTERNATIONAL

Baia della Fontanella, Isola D'Elba, 57031 Marina di Capoliveri (LI), Italy

Tel: +39 0565 946111 **Fax:** +39 0565 946662

e-mail: hotel@elbainternational.com

HOTEL J AND J

Via di Mezzo 20, 50121 Florence, Italy

Tel: +39 055 263121 **Fax:** +39 055 240282

e-mail: jandj@dada.it

VILLA MONTARTINO

Via Gherardo Silvani 151, 50125 Florence, Italy

Tel: +39 055 223520 **Fax:** +39 055 223495

e-mail: info@montartino.com

HOTEL VILLA ARISTON

Viale C. Colombo 355, 55043 Lido Di Camaiore – Lucca, Italy

Tel: +39 0584 610633 **Fax:** +39 0584 610631

e-mail: info@villaariston.it

HOTEL MONTERIGGIONI

Via 1 Maggio 4, 53035 Monteriggioni, Italy

Tel: +39 0577 305009 **Fax:** +39 0577 305011

e-mail: info@hotelmonteriggioni.net

CASTEL PIETRAIO

Strada Di Strove 33, 53035 Monteriggioni, Italy

Tel: +39 0577 300020 **Fax:** +39 0577 300977

e-mail: castelpietraio@tin.it

HOTEL RELAIS LA SUVERA

53030 Pievescola – Siena, Italy

Tel: +39 0577 960300 **Fax:** +39 0577 960220

e-mail: lasuvera@lasuvera.it

IL PELLICANO

58018 Porto Ercole (Gr), Tuscany, Italy

Tel: +39 0564 858111 **Fax:** +39 0564 833418

e-mail: info@pellicanohotel.com

HOTEL TORRE DI CALA PICCOLA

Porto Santo Stefano, 58019 Argentario, Italy

Tel: +39 0564 825111 **Fax:** +39 0564 825235

e-mail: prenotazioni@torredicalapiccola.com

HOTEL CALA DEL PORTO

Via Del Pozzo, 58040 Punta Ala, Italy

Tel: +39 0564 922455 **Fax:** +39 0564 920716

e-mail: cala.puntaala@baglionihotels.com

PALAZZO LEOPOLDO

Via Roma 33, 53017 Radda In Chianti, Italy

Tel: +39 0577 735605 **Fax:** +39 0577 738031

e-mail: leopoldo@chiantinet.it

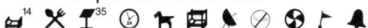

HOTEL CERTOSA DI MAGGIANO

Strada Di Certosa 82, 53100 Siena, Italy

Tel: +39 0577 288180 **Fax:** +39 0577 288189

e-mail: info@certosadimaggiano.it

ROMANTIK HOTEL LE SILVE DI ARMENZANO

06081 Loc. Armenzano, Assisi (PG), Italy

Tel: +39 075 801 9000 **Fax:** +39 075 801 9005

e-mail: hotellesilve@tin.it

ROMANTIK HOTEL VILLA DI MONTE SOLARE

Via Montali 7, 06070 Colle San Paolo - Panicale (PG), Italy

Tel: +39 075 832376 **Fax:** +39 075 8355818

e-mail: info@villamontesolare.it

CASTELLO DI PETROIA

Località Petroia, 06020 Gubbio (Pg), Italy

Tel: +39 075 92 02 87 / 92 01 09 **Fax:** +39 075 92 01 08

e-mail: castellodipetroia@castellodipetroia.com

CASTELLO DELL'OSCANO HISTORICAL RESIDENCE

06134 Perugia, Localita Cenerente, Italy

Tel: +39 075 584371 **Fax:** +39 075 692666

e-mail: info@oscano.com

VILLA DI PIAZZANO

Località Piazzano, 06069 Tuoro Sul Trasimeno (PG), Italy

Tel: +39 075 826226 **Fax:** +39 075 826336

e-mail: info@villadipiazzano.com

VILLA MILANI - RESIDENZA D'EPOCA

Loc. Colle Attivoli 4, 06049 Spoleto, Italy

Tel: +39 0743 225056 **Fax:** +39 0743 49824

e-mail: info@villamilani.com

HOTEL BRAMANTE

Via Orvietana 48, 06059 Todi (PG), Italy

Tel: +39 075 8948381/2/3 **Fax:** +39 075 8948074

e-mail: bramante@hotelbramante.it

Hotel Ca' Sette

Via Cunizza Da Romano 4, 36061 Bassano del Grappa, Italy

Tel: +39 0424 383350 **Fax:** +39 0424 393287

e-mail: info@ca-sette.it

Park Hotel Brasilia

Via Levantina, 30017 Lido Di Jesolo, Italy

Tel: +39 0421 380851 **Fax:** +39 0421 92244

e-mail: info@parkhotelbrasilia.com

Hotel Villa Condulmer

Via Preganziol 1, 31020 Mogliano Veneto, Italy

Tel: +39 041 5972 700 **Fax:** +39 041 5972 777

e-mail: info@hvc.ve.it

Relais La Magioca

Via Moron 3, 37024 Negrar (Verona), Italy

Tel: +39 045 600 0167 **Fax:** +39 045 600 0840

e-mail: info@magioca.it

Casa Belmonte Relais

Via Belmonte 2, 36030 Sarcedo, Italy

Tel: +39 0445 884833 **Fax:** +39 0445884 134

e-mail: info@casabelmonte.com

Hotel Giorgione

SS. Apostoli 4587, 30131 Venice, Italy

Tel: +39 041 522 5810 **Fax:** +39 041 523 9092

e-mail: giorgione@hotelgiorgione.com

ALBERGO QUATTRO FONTANE

30126 Lido Di Venezia, Venice, Italy

Tel: +39 041 526 0227 **Fax:** +39 041 526 0726

e-mail: quafonve@tin.it

Luxembourg

LUXEMBOURG (REMICH)

HOTEL SAINT~NICOLAS

31 Esplanade, 5533 Remich, Luxembourg

Tel: +352 2666 3 **Fax:** +352 2666 3666

e-mail: hotel@pt.lu

Monaco

MONACO (MONTE~CARLO)

MONTE~CARLO BEACH HOTEL

Avenue Princesse Grace, 06190 Roquebrune – Cap~Martin, France

Tel: +377 92 16 25 25 **Fax:** +377 92 16 26 26

e-mail: resort@sbm.mc

The Netherlands

AMBASSADE HOTEL

Herengracht 341, 1016 Az Amsterdam, The Netherlands

Tel: +31 20 5550222 **Fax:** +31 20 5550277

e-mail: info@ambassade-hotel.nl

BLAKES

Keizersgracht 384, 1016 GB Amsterdam, The Netherlands

Tel: +31 20 530 20 10 **Fax:** +31 20 530 20 30

e-mail: hotel@blakes.nl

SEVEN ONE SEVEN

Prinsengracht 717, 1017 Jw Amsterdam, The Netherlands

Tel: +31 20 42 70 717 **Fax:** +31 20 42 30 717

e-mail: info@717hotel.nl

HOTEL DE HOLTWEIJDE

Spiekweg 7, 7635 Lattrop, The Netherlands

Tel: +31 541 229 234 **Fax:** +31 541 22 94 45

e-mail: info@holtweijde.nl

CHÂTEAU ST GERLACH

Joseph Corneli Allée 1, 6301 KK Valkenburg A/D Geul, Maastricht, The Netherlands

Tel: +31 43 608 88 88 **Fax:** +31 43 604 28 83

e-mail: reservations@stgerlach.chateauhotels.nl

HOTEL DE WIEMSEL

Winhofflaan 2, 7631 Hx Ootmarsum, The Netherlands

Tel: +31 541 292 155 **Fax:** +31 541 293 295

e-mail: info@wiemsel.nl

Norway

KONGSVOLD FJELDSTUE

Dovrefjell, 7340 Oppdal, Norway

Tel: +47 72 40 43 40 **Fax:** +47 72 40 43 41

e-mail: post@kongsvold.no

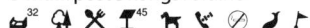

HOTEL BASTION

Skippergaten 7, 0152 Oslo, Norway

Tel: +47 22 47 77 00 **Fax:** +47 22 33 11 80

e-mail: booking@hotelbastion.no

WALAKER HOTELL

6879 Solvorn, Sogn, Norway

Tel: +47 576 82080 **Fax:** +47 576 82081

e-mail: hotel@walaker.com

FLEISCHERS HOTEL

5700 Voss, Norway

Tel: +47 56 52 05 00 **Fax:** +47 56 52 05 01

e-mail: hotel@fleischers.no

Portugal

CONVENTO DE SÃO PAULO

Aldeia Da Serra, 7170 –120 Redondo, Portugal

Tel: +351 266 989160 **Fax:** +351 266 999104

e-mail: hotelconvspaulo@mail.telepac.pt

ROMANTIK HOTEL VIVENDA MIRANDA

Porto de Mós, 8600 Lagos, Portugal

Tel: +351 282 763222 **Fax:** +351 282 760342

e-mail: reservations@vivendamiranda.pt

SOLAR DO CASTELO

Rua das Cozinhas 2, 1100–181 Lisbon, Portugal

Tel: +351 218 870 909 **Fax:** +351 218 870 907

e-mail: solar.castelo@heritage.pt

TIVOLI HOTEL PALÁCIO DE SETEAIS

Rua Barbosa de Bocage, 10, Seteais, 2710 Sintra, Portugal

Tel: +351 219 233 200 **Fax:** +351 219 234 277

e-mail: hpseteais@mail.telepac.pt

QUINTA DA BELA VISTA

Caminho do Avista Navios 4, 9000 Funchal, Madeira, Portugal

Tel: +351 291 706400 **Fax:** +351 291 706411

Quinta das Vistas Palacio Gardens

Caminho de Santo Antonio 52, 9000-187 Funchal, Madeira, Portugal

Tel: +351 291 750 007 **Fax:** +351 291 750 017

e-mail: info@charminghotelsmadeira.com

Quinta do Estreito

Rua José Joaquim da Costa, Estreito de Câmara De Lobos, 9325–034 Madeira, Portugal

Tel: +351 291 910530 **Fax:** +351 291 910549

e-mail: quintaestreito@charminghotelsmadeira.com

Quinta do Monte

Caminho do Monte 192, 9050-288 Funchal, Madeira, Portugal

Tel: +351 291 780 100 **Fax:** +351 291 780 110

e-mail: info@quintadomonte.com

Quinta Perestrello

Rua do Dr. Pita 3, 9000-089 Funchal, Madeira, Portugal

Tel: +351 291 706700 **Fax:** +351 291 706706

e-mail: quintaperestrello@charminghotelsmadeira.com

Vintage House Hotel

Lugar da Ponte, 5085-034 Pinhão, Portugal

Tel: +351 254 730 230 **Fax:** +351 254 730 238

e-mail: vintagehouse@hotelvintagehouse.com

Spain

Hotel Antequera Golf

Sta Catalina S/N, 29200 Antequera, Spain

Tel: +34 95 27 04 531 **Fax:** +34 95 28 45 232

e-mail: comercial@hotelantequera.com

Hacienda El Santiscal

Avda. El Santiscal 129 (Lago De Arcos), 11630 Arcos de La Frontera, Spain

Tel: +34 956 70 83 13 **Fax:** +34 956 70 82 68

e-mail: santiscal@gadesinfo.com

Amanhavis Hotel

Calle del Pilar 3, 29679 Benahavis, Marbella, Spain

Tel: +34 952 85 60 26 **Fax:** +34 952 85 61 51

e-mail: info@amanhavis.com

El Cortijo de Los Mimbrales

Ctra del Rocio - Matalascañas, Km 30, 21750 Almonte (Huelva), Spain

Tel: +34 959 44 22 37 **Fax:** +34 959 44 24 43

e-mail: info@cortijomimbrales.com

Hotel La Bobadilla

Finca La Bobadilla, Apto. 144, 18300 Loja, Granada, Spain

Tel: +34 958 32 18 61 **Fax:** +34 958 32 18 10

e-mail: info@la-bobadilla.com

HOTEL VILLA JEREZ

Avda. de La Cruz Roja 7, 11407 Jerez de La Frontera, Spain

Tel: +34 956 15 31 00 **Fax:** +34 956 30 43 00

e-mail: reservas@villajerez.com

HOTEL LA CASONA DE LA CIUDAD ****

C/Marqués de Salvatierra 5, 29400 Ronda, Málaga, Spain

Tel: +34 952 87 95 95/96 **Fax:** +34 952 16 10 95

e-mail: reservas@lacasonadelaciudad.com

HOTEL LA FUENTE DE LA HIGUERA

Partido de Los Frontones, 29400 Ronda, Málaga, Spain

Tel: +34 95 2 11 43 55 **Fax:** +34 95 2 11 43 56

e-mail: info@hotellafuente.com

LA POSADA DEL TORCAL

29230 Villanueva de La Concepción, Málaga, Spain

Tel: +34 952 03 11 77 **Fax:** +34 952 03 10 06

e-mail: posada-torcal@codesort.net

EL MOLINO DE SANTILLÁN

Ctra. de Macharaviaya, Km 3, 29730 Rincón de La Victoria, Málaga, Spain

Tel: +34 952 40 09 49 **Fax:** +34 952 40 09 50

e-mail: msantillan@spa.es

LAS DUNAS BEACH HOTEL & SPA

La Boladilla Baja, Crta. de Cádiz Km 163.5, 29689 Marbella – Estepona (Málaga), Spain

Tel: +34 952 79 43 45 **Fax:** +34 952 79 48 25

e-mail: lasdunas@las–dunas.com

Hotel Byblos Andaluz

Mijas Golf, 29650 Mijas~Costa, Málaga, Spain

Tel: +34 952 47 30 50 **Fax:** +34 952 58 63 27

e-mail: comerical@byblos-andaluz.com

Cortijo El Esparragal

Ctra. de Merida, KM 795, 41860 Gerena (Sevilla), Spain

Tel: +34 955 78 27 02 **Fax:** +34 955 78 27 83

e-mail: elesparragal@elesparragal.com

Hacienda Benazuza El Bulli Hotel

41800 Sanlúcar La Mayor, Seville, Spain

Tel: +34 955 70 33 44 **Fax:** +34 955 70 34 10

e-mail: hbenazuza@elbullihotel.com.

Hotel Cortijo Águila Real

Ctra. Guillena–Burguillos Km 4, 41210 Guillena, Sevilla, Spain

Tel: +34 955 78 50 06 **Fax:** +34 955 78 43 30

e-mail: hotel@aguilareal.com

Hotel Hacienda La Boticaria

Ctra. Alcalá - Utrera Km.2, 41500 Alcalá de Guadaira, Sevilla, Spain

Tel: +34 955 69 88 20 **Fax:** +34 955 69 87 55

e-mail: info@laboticaria-hotel.com

Palacio Marqués de la Gomera

C/ San Pedro 20, 41640 Osuna, Sevilla, Spain

Tel: +34 95 4 81 22 23 **Fax:** +34 95 4 81 02 00

e-mail: palaciogomera@telefonica.net

PALACIO DE SAN BENITO

c/San Benito S/N, 41370 Cazalla de La Sierra, Sevilla, Spain

Tel: +34 954 88 33 36 **Fax:** +34 954 88 31 62

ALMENARA GOLF HOTEL & SPA

Avenida Almenara, 11310 Sotogrande, Spain

Tel: + 34 956 58 20 00 **Fax:** +34 956 58 20 01

e-mail: nhalmenara@hotels.com

LA PARADA DEL COMPTE

Antigua Estación de Ferrocarril, 44597 Torre del Compte, Teruel, Spain

Tel: +34 978 76 90 72 **Fax:** +34 978 76 90 74

PALACIO DE CUTRE

La Goleta S/N Villamayor, 33583 Infiesto, Asturias, Spain

Tel: +34 985 70 80 72 **Fax:** +34 985 70 80 19

e-mail: hotel@palaciodecutre.com

CAS GASI

Apdo. Correos 117, 07814 Santa Gertrudis, Ibiza, Balearic Islands.

Tel: +34 971 197 700 **Fax:** +34 971 197 899

e-mail: info@casgasi.com

CA'S XORC

Carretera de Deía, Km 56,1 07100 Sóller, Mallorca, Balearic Islands

Tel: +34 971 63 82 80 **Fax:** +34 971 63 29 49

e-mail: stay@casxorc.com

CAN FURIÓS PETIT HOTEL

Cami Vell Binibona 11, Binibona, 07314 Caimari, Mallorca, Balearic Islands

Tel:+34 971 51 57 51 **Fax:**+34 971 87 53 66

e-mail: info@can-furios.com

HOTEL MONNABER NOU

Possessió Monnaber Nou, 07310 Campanet, Mallorca, Balearic Islands

Tel:+34 971 87 71 76 **Fax:**+34 971 87 71 27

e-mail: info@monnaber.com

HOTEL VISTAMAR DE VALLDEMOSSA

Ctra Valldemossa, Andratx Km. 2, 07170 Valldemossa, Mallorca, Balearic Islands

Tel:+34 971 61 23 00 **Fax:**+34 971 61 25 83

e-mail: info@vistamarhotel.es

READ'S

Ca'N Moragues, 07320 Santa María, Mallorca, Balearic Islands

Tel:+34 971 14 02 62 **Fax:**+34 971 14 07 62

e-mail: readshotel@readshotel.com

SA POSADA D'AUMALLIA

Camino Son Prohens 1027, 07200 Felanitx, Mallorca, Balearic Islands

Tel:+34 971 58 26 57 **Fax:**+34 971 58 32 69

e-mail: aumallia@aumallia.com

SCOTT'S

Plaza de La Iglesia 12, 07350 Binissalem, Mallorca, Balearic Islands

Tel:+34 971 87 01 00 **Fax:**+34 971 87 02 67

e-mail: reserve@scottshotel.com

ELBA PALACE GOLF HOTEL

Urb. Fuerteventura Golf Club, Carretera de Jandia, km11, 35610
Antigua, Fuerteventura.

Tel: +34 928 16 39 22 **Fax:** +34 928 16 39 23

e-mail: epg@hoteleselba.com

GRAN HOTEL COSTA MELONERAS ★★★★

C/Mar Mediterráneo 1, 35100 Maspalomas, Gran Canaria, Canary
Islands

Tel: +34 928 12 81 00 **Fax:** +34 928 12 81 22

e-mail: info@ghcmeloneras.com

FINCA DE LAS SALINAS

C/ La Cuesta 17, 35570 Yaiza, Lanzarote, Canary Islands

Tel: +34 928 83 03 25 **Fax:** +34 928 83 03 29

e-mail: Fsalina@santandersupernet.com

GRAN MELIÁ VOLCÁN

Urb. Castillo del Aguila, Playa Blanco, Lanzarote, Canary Islands

Tel: +34 928 51 91 85 **Fax:** +34 928 51 91 32

e-mail: gran.melia.volcan.lanzarote@solmelia.com

GRAN HOTEL BAHÍA DEL DUQUE RESORT

38660 Adeje, Costa Adeje, Tenerife South, Canary Islands

Tel: +34 922 74 69 33/34 **Fax:** +34 922 74 69 25

e-mail: comercial@bahia-duque.com

HOTEL BOTÁNICO ★★★★★GL

Avda. Richard J. Yeoward, Urb. Botánico, 38400 Puerto de La Cruz,
Tenerife, Canary Islands

Tel: +34 922 38 14 00 **Fax:** +34 922 38 39 93

e-mail: hotelbotanico@hotelbotanico.com

Hotel Jardín Tropical

Calle Gran Bretaña, 38670 Costa Adeje, Tenerife, Canary Islands

Tel: +34 922 74 60 00 **Fax:** +34 922 74 60 60

e-mail: hotel@jardin–tropical.com

SPAIN / CANTABRIA (VILLACARRIEDO)

Palacio de Soñanes

Bomo Quintanal 1, Villacarriedo, Cantabria, Spain

Tel: +34 942 59 06 00 **Fax:** +34 942 59 06 14

e-mail: informacion@palaciodevillacarriedo.com

SPAIN / CASTILLA~LA MANCHA (ALMAGRO)

La Casa del Rector

c/Pedro Oviedo 8, 13270 Almagro, Ciudad Real, Spain

Tel: +34 926 26 12 59 **Fax:** +34 926 26 12 60

e-mail: recepcion@lacasadelrector.com

SPAIN / CASTILLA Y LEÓN (ÁVILA)

El Milano Real

C/ Toleo S/N, Hoyos del Espino, 05634 Ávila, Spain

Tel: +34 920 349 108 **Fax:** +34 920 349 156

e-mail: info@elmilanoreal.com

SPAIN / CASTILLA Y LEÓN (SALAMANCA)

Hotel Rector

Rector Esperabé 10–Apartado 399, 37008 Salamanca, Spain

Tel: +34 923 21 84 82 **Fax:** +34 923 21 40 08

e-mail: hotelrector@telefonica.net

SPAIN / CASTILLA Y LEÓN (SEGOVIA)

Caserío de Lobones

Valverde del Majano, 40140 Segovia, Spain

Tel: +34 921 12 84 08 **Fax:** +34 921 12 83 44

HOTEL CLARIS

Pau Claris 150, 08009 Barcelona, Spain

Tel: +34 934 87 62 62 **Fax:** +34 932 15 79 70

e-mail: claris@derbyhotels.es

HOTEL COLÓN

Avenida de La Catedral 7, 08002 Barcelona, Spain

Tel: +34 933 01 14 04 **Fax:** +34 933 17 29 15

e-mail: comercial@hotelcolon.es

THE GALLERY

Rosselló 249, 08008 Barcelona, Spain

Tel: +34 934 15 99 11 **Fax:** +34 934 15 91 84

e-mail: email@galleryhotel.com

HOTEL RIGAT PARK

Playa de Fenals, 17310 Lloret de Mar, Costa Brava, Spain

Tel: +34 972 36 52 00 **Fax:** +34 972 37 04 11

e-mail: rigat@rigat.com

SPA

HOTEL GOLF PERALADA

C/ Rocaberti S/N, 17491 Peralada, Girona, Spain

Tel: +34 972 53 88 30 **Fax:** +34 972 53 88 07

e-mail: hotel@golfperalada.com

SPA

MAS FALGARONA

Avinyonet de Puigventos, 17742 Gerona, Spain

Tel: +34 972 54 66 28 **Fax:** +34 972 54 70 71

e-mail: email@masfalgarona.com

Hotel Estela Barcelona

Avda. Port d'Aiguadolç S/N, 08870 Sitges (Barcelona), Spain

Tel: +34 938 11 45 45 **Fax:** +34 938 11 45 46

e-mail: info@hotelestela.com

Hotel Termes Montbrió Resort, Spa & Park

Carrer Nou 38, 43340 Montbrió del Camp (Tarragona), Spain

Tel: +34 977 81 40 00 **Fax:** +34 977 82 69 69

e-mail: hoteltermes@gruprocblanc.com

Xalet La Coromina

Carretera de Vic S/N, 17406 Viladrau, Spain

Tel: +34 938 84 92 64 **Fax:** +34 938 84 81 60

e-mail: xaletcoromina@telelina.es

Antiguo Convento

C/ de Las Monjas, S/N Boadilla del Monte, 28660 Madrid, Spain.

Tel: + 34 91 632 22 20 **Fax:** +34 91 633 15 12

e-mail: informacion@elconvento.net

Hotel Villa Real

Plaza de Las Cortes 10, 28014 Madrid, Spain

Tel: +34 914 20 37 67 **Fax:** +34 914 20 25 47

e-mail: villareal@derbyhotels.es

Hyatt Regency La Manga

Los Belones, 30385 Cartagena, Murcia, Spain

Tel: +34 968 33 12 34 **Fax:** +34 968 33 12 35

e-mail: info@hyattlamanga.com

Hotel Buena Vista

Partida Tossalet 82, La Xara, 03709 Dénia, Spain

Tel: +34 965 78 79 95 **Fax:** +34 966 42 71 70

e-mail: hotelbuenavista@alc.servicom.es

SPAIN / VALENCIA (XÀTIVA)

Hotel Mont Sant

Subida Al Castillo, s/n Xàtiva, 46800 Valencia, Spain

Tel: +34 962 27 50 81 **Fax:** +34 962 28 19 05

e-mail: montsant@servidex.com

Sweden

SWEDEN (BORGHOLM)

Halltorps Gästgiveri

38792 Borgholm, Sweden

Tel: +46 485 85000 **Fax:** +46 485 85001

e-mail: halltorps.gastgiveri@mailbox.calypso.net

SWEDEN (HESTRA – SMÅLAND)

Hestravikens Wärdshus

Vik, 33027, Hestra, Småland, Sweden

Tel: +46 370 33 68 00 **Fax:** +46 370 33 62 90

e-mail: info@hestraviken.se

SWEDEN (LAGAN)

Romantik Hotel Toftaholm Herrgård

Toftaholm Pa, 34014 Lagan, Sweden

Tel: +46 370 440 55 **Fax:** +46 370 440 45

e-mail: frontoffice@toftaholmherrgard.com

HÄCKEBERGA MANOR

24013 Genarp, Sweden

Tel: +46 40 48 04 40 **Fax:** +46 40 48 04 02

e-mail: info@hackebergaslott.se

ROMANTIK HOTEL ÅKERBLADS

79370 Tällberg, Sweden

Tel: +46 247 50800 **Fax:** +46 247 50652

e-mail: info@akerblad-tallberg.se

Switzerland

HOSTELLERIE BON ACCUEIL

1837 Château d'Oex, Switzerland

Tel: +41 26 924 6320 **Fax:** +41 26 924 5126

e-mail: host–bon–accueil@bluewin.ch

LE GRAND CHALET

Neueretstrasse, 3780 Gstaad, Switzerland

Tel: +41 33 748 7676 **Fax:** +41 33 748 7677

e-mail: hotel@grandchalet.ch

ROYAL PARK ***** HOTEL

3718 Kandersteg, Bernese Oberland, Switzerland

Tel: +41 33 675 88 88 **Fax:** +41 33 675 88 80

e-mail: royal.ksteg@spectraweb.ch

Turkey

MARINA RESIDENCE & RESTAURANT

Mermerli Sokak No. 15, Kaleici, 07100 Antalya, Turkey

Tel: +90 242 247 5490 **Fax:** +90 242 241 1765

e-mail: marinahotel@superonline.com

OUTDOOR CENTRE RESORT

Gift Gesmeier Mevkii, Beldibi, Antalya, Turkey

Tel: +90 242 824 9666 **Fax:** +90 242 824 9393

e-mail: mail@turkeyoutdoors.com

RENAISSANCE ANTALYA RESORT

PO Box 654, 07004 Beldibi - Kemer, Antalya, Turkey

Tel: +90 242 824 84 31 **Fax:** +90 242 824 84 30

e-mail: renaissance@superonline.com

TALYA HOTEL

Fevzi Çakmak Caddesi No. 30, 07100 Antalya, Turkey

Tel: +90 242 248 6800 **Fax:** +90 242 241 5400

e-mail: info@talya.com.tr

TEKELI KONAKLARI

Dizdar Hasan Sokak, Kaleici, Antalya, Turkey

Tel: +90 242 244 54 65 **Fax:** +90 242 242 67 14

e-mail: mirya@superonline.com

TUVANA RESIDENCE

Tuzcular Mahallesi, Karanlik Sokak 7, 07100 Kaleiçi - Antalya, Turkey

Tel: +90 242 247 60 15 **Fax:** +90 242 241 19 81

e-mail: tuvanaotel@superonline.com

TURKEY (BODRUM)

DIVAN PALMIRA HOTEL

Kelesharim Cad 6, 48483 Türkbükü – Bodrum, Turkey

Tel: +90 252 377 5601 **Fax:** +90 252 377 5952

TURKEY (BODRUM)

L'AMBIANCE RESORT - BODRUM

Buyuk Iskender Yolu, Myndos Kapisi 48400, Bodrum – Mugla, Turkey

Tel: +90 252 313 83 30 **Fax:** +90 252 313 82 00

e-mail: info@lambiance.com

TURKEY (GÖREME – CAPPADOCIA)

CCS - CAPPADOCIA CAVE SUITES

Gafelli Mahallesi, unlü Sokak, 05180 Göreme – Nevsehir, Turkey

Tel: +90 384 271 2800 **Fax:** +90 384 271 27 99

e-mail: info@cappadociacavesuites.com

TURKEY (KALKAN)

HOTEL VILLA MAHAL

P.K. 4 Kalkan, 07960 Antalya, Turkey

Tel: +90 242 844 32 68 **Fax:** +90 242 844 21 22

e-mail: info@villamahal.com

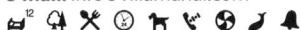

TURKEY (UGHISAR - CAPPADOCIA)

MUSEUM HOTEL

Tekelli Mahalesi 1, Uchisar - Nevsehir, Turkey

Tel: +90 384 219 22 20 **Fax:** +90 384 219 24 44

e-mail: info@museum-hotel.com

Ürgüp Evi

Esbelli Mahallesi 54, 5400 Ürgüp-Nevsehir, Turkey

Tel: +90 384 341 3173 **Fax:** +90 384 341 6269

e-mail: faruk@urgupeui.com.tr

Hotel Bellapais Gardens

Crusader Road, Bellapais, Girne, Northern Cyprus

Tel: +90 392 815 60 66 **Fax:** +90 392 815 76 67

e-mail: info@bellapaisgardens.com

The Hideaway Club

Karaman Road, Edremit, Girne, Northen Cyprus

Tel: +90 392 822 2620 **Fax:** +90 392 822 3133

e-mail: hideaway@kktc.net

North America, Bermuda, Caribbean, Mexcio & Pacifc

United States of America

ARIZONA - SEDONA
Canyon Villa Inn

125 Canyon Circle Drive, Sedona, Arizona 86351

Tel: 1 520 284 1226 **Fax:** 1 520 284 2114

e-mail: canvilla@sedona.net

ARIZONA - SEDONA
L'Auberge De Sedona

L'Auberge Lane, PO Box B, Sedona, Arizona 86339

Tel: 1 928 282 1661 **Fax:** 1 928 282 2885

ARIZONA - TUCSON
Tanque Verde Ranch

14301 East Speedway, Tucson, Arizona 85748

Tel: 1 520 296 6275 **Fax:** 1 520 721 9426

e-mail: dude@tvgr.com

ARIZONA - TUCSON
White Stallion Ranch

9251 West Twin Peaks Road, Tucson, Arizona 85743

Tel: 1 520 297 0252 **Fax:** 1 520 744 2786

e-mail: info@wsranch.com

Carter House

301 L Street, Eureka, California 95501

Tel: 1 707 444 8062 **Fax:** 1 707 444 8067

e-mail: 301.wines.com/wines

Gingerbread Mansion Inn

P.O.Box 40; 400 Berding Street, Ferndale, California 95536

Tel: 1 707 786 4000   **Fax:** 1 707 786 4381

e-mail: innkeeper@gingerbread-mansion.com

The Bed & Breakfast Inn At La Jolla

7753 Draper Avenue, La Jolla, California 92037

Tel: 1 858 456 2066 **Fax:** 1 858 456 1510

Mill Valley Inn

165 Throckmorton Avenue, Mill Valley, California 94941

Tel: 1 415 389 6608 **Fax:** 1 415 389 5051

e-mail: mgr@millvalleyinn.com

Doryman's Inn

2102 West Ocean Front, Newport Beach, California 92663

Tel: 1 949 675 7300 **Fax:** 1 949 675 7300

e-mail: info@21oceanfront.com

Shadow Mountain Resort & Club

45750 San Luis Rey, Palm Desert, California 92260

Tel: 1 760 346 6123 **Fax:** 1 760 346 6518

e-mail: res@shadow-mountain.com

CALIENTE TROPICS RESORT

411 EAST PALM CANYON DRIVE, PALM SPRINGS, CALIFORNIA 92264

Tel: 1 760 327 1391 **Fax:** 1 760 318 1883

e-mail: info@Calientetropics.com

L'HORIZON

1050 East Palm Canyon Drive, Palm Springs, California 92264

Tel: 1 760 323 1858 **Fax:** 1 760 327 2933

e-mail: hotelslhorizon@palmsprings.com

THE WILLOWS

412 West Tahquitz Canyon Way, Palm Springs, California 92262

Tel: 1 760 320 0771 **Fax:** 1 760 320 0780

e-mail: innkeeper@thewillowspalmsprings.com

NOB HILL LAMBOURNE

725 Pine Street, San Francisco, California 94108

Tel: 1 415 433 2287 **Fax:** 1 415 433 0975

e-mail: nhl@jdvhospitality.com

SPA

GERSTLE PARK INN

34 Grove Street, San Rafael, California 94901

Tel: 1 415 721 7611 **Fax:** 1 415 721 7600

e-mail: innkeeper@gerstleparkinn.com

WOOLLEY'S PETITE SUITES

2721 Hotel Terrace Road, Santa Ana, California 92705

Tel: 1 714 540 1111 **Fax:** 1 714 662 1643

e-mail: wps@petitesuites.com

Upham Hotel

1404 De La Vina Street, Santa Barbara, California 93101

Tel: 1 805 962 0058 **Fax:** 1 805 963 2825

e-mail: upham.hotel@verizon.net

The Georgian Hotel

1415 Ocean Avenue, Santa Monica, California 90405

Tel: 1 310 395 9945 **Fax:** 1 310 451 3374

e-mail: sales@georgianhotel.com

Waters Edge Hotel

25 Main Street, Tiburon, California 94920

Tel: 1 415 789 5999 **Fax:** 1 415 789 5888

e-mail: watersedgehotel@jdvhospitality.com

The Inn at Beaver Creek

10 Elk Track Lane, Beaver Creek Resort, Colorado, 81620

Tel: 1 970 845 5990   **Fax:** 1 970 845 6204

e-mail: vbcrp@vailresorts.com

Castle Marne

1572 Race Street, Denver, Colorado 80206

Tel: 1 303 331 0621 **Fax:** 1 303 331 0623

e-mail: info@castlemarne.com

The Stanley Hotel

333 Wonderview Avenue, PO Box 1767, Estes Park, Colorado. 80517

Tel: 1 970 586 3371 **Fax:** 1 970 586 4964

THE CLIFF HOUSE AT PIKES PEAK

306 Cañon Avenue, Manitou Springs, Colorado 80829

Tel: 1 719 685 3000 **Fax:** 1 719 685 3913

e-mail: information@thecliffhouse.com

VISTA VERDE GUEST RANCH

PO Box 770465, Steamboat Springs, Colorado 80477

Tel: 1 970 879 3858 **Fax:** 1 970 879 1413

e-mail: reservations@vistaverde.com

SONNENALP RESORT OF VAIL

20 Vail Road, Vail, Colorado 81657

Tel: 1 970 476 5656 **Fax:** 1 970 476 1639

e-mail: info@sonnenalp.com

BOARDWALK PLAZA HOTEL

Olive Avenue & The Boardwalk, Rehoboth Beach, Delaware 19971

Tel: 1 302 227 7169 **Fax:** 1 302 227 0561

e-mail: bph@boardwalkplaza.com

THE SUNDY HOUSE RESORT

106 South Swinton Avenue, Delray Beach, Florida 33444

Tel: 1 561 272 5678 **Fax:** 1 561 272 1115

SIMONTON COURT HISTORIC INN & COTTAGES

320 Simonton Street, Key West, Florida 33040

Tel: 1 305 294 6386 **Fax:** 1 305 293 8446

e-mail: simontoncourt@aol.com

THE INN AT FISHER ISLAND

one Fisher Island Drive, Miami Beach, Florida 33109

Tel: 1 305 535 6080 **Fax:** 1 305 535 6003

e-mail: hotel@fisherisland.com

HOTEL ESCALANTE

290 Fifth Avenue South, Naples, Florida 34102

Tel: 1 941 659 3466 **Fax:** 1 941 262 8748

HENDERSON VILLAGE

125 South Langston Circle, Perry, Georgia 31069

Tel: 1 478 988 8696   **Fax:** 1 478 988 9009

e-mail: info@hendersonvillage.com

THE ELIZA THOMPSON HOUSE

5 West Jones Street, Savannah, Georgia 31401

Tel: 1 912 236 3620   **Fax:** 1 912 238 1920

e-mail: innkeeper@elizathompsonhouse.com

GRANITE STEPS

126 East Gaston Street, Savannah, Georgia 31401

Tel: 1 912 233 5380   **Fax:** 1 912 236 3116

THE PRESIDENT'S QUARTERS

225 East President Street, Savannah, Georgia 31401

Tel: 1 912 233 1600 **Fax:** 1 912 238 0849

THE SUTTON PLACE HOTEL

21 East Bellevue Place, Chicago, Illinois 60611

Tel: 1 312 266 2100 **Fax:** 1 312 266 2103

e-mail: info_chi@suttonplace.com

MADEWOOD PLANTATION HOUSE

4250 Highway 308, Napoleanville,Louisiana 70390

Tel: 1 985 369 7151 **Fax:** 1 985 369 9848

e-mail: madewoodpl@aol.com

HOTEL MAISON DE VILLE

727 Rue Toulouse, New Orleans, Louisiana 70130

Tel: 1 504 561 5858 **Fax:** 1 504 528 9939

e-mail: tyoung@dal.meristar.com

THE ANNAPOLIS INN

144 Prince George Street, Annapolis, Maryland 21401-1723

Tel: 1 410 295 5200 **Fax:** 1 410 295 5201

e-mail: info@annapolisinn.com

ANTRIM 1844

30 Trevanion Rd, Taneytown, Maryland 21787

Tel: 1 410 756 6812 **Fax:** 1 410 756 2744

e-mail: antrim1844@erols.com

THE GEORGE WASHINGTON UNIVERSITY INN

824 New Hampshire Avenue, N.W. Washington D.C., District of Columbia 20037

Tel: 1 202 337 6620 **Fax:** 1 202 298 7499

e-mail: info@gwuinn.com

Green Oaks

580 Beach Boulevard, Biloxi, Mississippi 39530

Tel: 1 228 436 6257 **Fax:** 1 228 436 6225

e-mail: greenoaks4@aol.com

Fairview Inn

734 Fairview Street, Jackson, Mississippi 39202

Tel: 1 601 948 3429 **Fax:** 1 601 948 1203

e-mail: fairview@fairviewinn.com

Dunleith Plantation

84 Homochitto Street, Natchez, Mississippi, 39120

Tel: 1 601 446 8500 **Fax:** 1 601 446 8554

e-mail: Dunleith@bkbank.com

Monmouth Plantation

36 Melrose Avenue At, John A Quitman Parkway, Natchez, Mississippi 39120

Tel: 1 601 442 5852 **Fax:** 1 601 446 7762

e-mail: luxury@monmouthplantation.com

Anchuca Historic Mansion & Inn

1010 First East Street, Vicksburg, Mississippi 39183

Tel: 1 601 661 0111 **Fax:** 1 601 661 0111

e-mail: Reservation@AnchucaMansion.com

The Duff Green Mansion

1114 First East Street, Vicksburg, Mississippi 39180

Tel: 1 601 636 6968 **Fax:** 1 601 661 0079

Chase Park Plaza Hotel

212 North Kingshighway Boulevard, St Louis, Missouri 63108

Tel: 1 314 633 3000 **Fax:** 1 314 633 1133

Copper Beech Inn

46 Main Street, Ivoryton, Connecticut 06442

Tel: 1 860 767 0330

The Inn at Mystic

US1 & State 27, PO Box 216, Mystic, Connecticut 06355

Tel: 1 860 536 9604 **Fax:** 1 860 572 1635

Stonecroft Country Inn

515 Pumpkin Hill Road, Ledyard, Connecticut 06339

Tel: 1 860 572 0771 **Fax:** 1 860 572 9161

e-mail: innkeeper@stonecroft.com

The Boulders Inn

East Shore Road, Route 45, New Preston, Connecticut 06777

Tel: 1 860 868 0541 **Fax:** 1 860 868 1925

e-mail: boulders@bouldersinn.com

The Old Mystic Inn

52 Main Street, Old Mystic, Connecticut 06372-0733

Tel: 1 860 572 9422 **Fax:** 1 860 572 9954

e-mail: omysticinn@aol.com

WEST LANE INN

22 West Lane, Ridgefield, Connecticut 06877

Tel: 1 203 438 7323 **Fax:** 1 203 438 7325

BLACKBERRY INN

82 Elm Street, Camden, Maine 04843

Tel: 1 207 236 6060 **Fax:** 1 207 236 9032

e-mail: blkberry@midcoast.com

CAMDEN MAINE STAY

22 High Street, Camden, Maine 04843

Tel: 1 207 236 9636 **Fax:** 1 207 236 0621

e-mail: innkeeper@camdenmainestay.com

HARTSTONE INN

41 Elm Street, Camden, Maine, 04843

Tel: 1 207 236 4259 **Fax:** 1 207 236 9575

e-mail: info@hartstoneinn.com

THE LODGE AT MOOSEHEAD LAKE

Upon Lily Bay Road, Box 1167, Greenville, Maine 04441

Tel: 1 207 695 4400 **Fax:** 1 207 695 2281

e-mail: innkeeper@lodgeatmooseheadlake.com

THE CAPTAIN LORD MANSION

6 Pleasant Street, Kennebunkport, Maine 04046-0800

Tel: 1 207 967 3141

e-mail: innkeeper@captainlord.com

GREENVILLE INN

Po Box 1194, Norris Street, Greenville, Maine 04441

Tel: 1 207 695 2206 **Fax:** 1 207 695 0335

e-mail: gvlinn@moosehead.net

THE NEWCASTLE INN

60 River Road, Newcastle, Maine 04553

Tel: 1 207 563 5685 **Fax:** 1 207 563 6877

e-mail: innkeep@newcastleinn.com

CAPTAIN LINDSEY HOUSE

5 Lindsey Street, Rockland, Maine 04841

Tel: 1 207 596 7950 **Fax:** 1 207 596 2758

e-mail: lindsey@midcoast.com

A CAMBRIDGE HOUSE

2218 Massachusetts Avenue, Cambridge, Massachusetts 02140–1836

Tel: 1 617 491 6300 **Fax:** 1 617 868 2848

e-mail: InnACH@aol.com

THE CHARLES STREET INN

94 Charles Street, Boston, Massachusetts 02114–4643

Tel: 1 617 314 8900 **Fax:** 1 617 371 0009

THE LENOX HOTEL

710 Boylston Street, Boston, Massachusetts 02116-2699

Tel: 1 617 536 5300 **Fax:** 1 617 236 0351

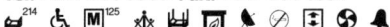

THE CAPTAIN'S HOUSE INN

369–377 Old Harbor Road, Chatham, Cape Cod, Massachusetts 02633

Tel: 1 508 945 0127 **Fax:** 1 508 945 0866

e-mail: info@captainshouseinn.com

WEDGEWOOD INN

83 Main Street, Route 6A, Yarmouth Port, Massachusetts 02675

Tel: 1 508 362 5157 **Fax:** 1 508 362 5851

e-mail: info@wedgewood–inn.com

THE WHALEWALK INN

220 Bridge Road, Eastham (Cape Cod), Massachusetts 02642

Tel: 1 508 255 0617 **Fax:** 1 508 240 0017

e-mail: information@whalewalkinn.com

DEERFIELD INN

81 Old Main Street, Deerfield, Massachusetts 01342-0305

Tel: 1 413 774 5587 **Fax:** 1 413 775 7221

e-mail: frontdesk@deerfieldinn.com

WHEATLEIGH

Hawthorne Road, Lenox, Massachusetts 01240

Tel: 1 413 637 0610 **Fax:** 1 413 637 4507

THE HARBOR LIGHT INN

58 Washington Street, Marblehead, Massachusetts 01945

Tel: 1 781 631 2186 **Fax:** 1 781 631 2216

Hob Knob Inn

128 Main Street, po box 239, Edgartown, Massachusetts 02539

Tel: 1 508 627 9510 **Fax:** 1 508 627 4560

e-mail: hobknob@hobknob.com

Thorncroft Inn

460 Main Street, PO Box 1022, Vineyard Haven, Massachusetts 02568

Tel: 1 508 693 3333 **Fax:** 1 508 693 5419

e-mail: innkeeper@thorncroft.com

The Victorian Inn

24 South Water Street, Edgartown, Massachusetts 02539

Tel: 1 508 627 4784

e-mail: victorianinn@vineyard.net

The Pineapple Inn

10 Hussey Street, Nantucket, Massachusetts 02554

Tel: 1 508 228 9992 **Fax:** 1 508 325 6051

e-mail: info@pineappleinn.com

Union Street Inn

7 Union Street, Nantucket, Massachusetts 02554

Tel: 1 508 228 9222 **Fax:** 1 508 325 0848

e-mail: unioninn@nantucket.net

Seacrest Manor

99 Marmion Way, Rockport, Massachusetts 01966

Tel: 1 978 546 2211

Chesterfield Inn

Route 9, PO Box 155, Chesterfield, New Hampshire 03443-0155

Tel: 1 603 256 3211 **Fax:** 1 603 256 6131

e-mail: chstinn@sover.net

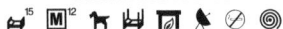

The Manor on Golden Pond

Route 3, PO Box T, Holderness, New Hampshire 03245

Tel: 1 603 968 3348 **Fax:** 1 603 968 2116

e-mail: info@manorongoldenpond.com

The Inn at Thorn Hill

Thorn Hill Road, Jackson Village, New Hampshire 03846

Tel: 1 603 383 4242

e-mail: thornhll@ncia.net

The Atlantic Inn

Po Box 1788, Block Island, Rhode Island 02807

Tel: 1 401 466 5883 **Fax:** 1 401 466 5678

e-mail: atlanticinn@iebiri.com

Cliffside Inn

2 Seaview Avenue, Newport, Rhode Island 02840

Tel: 1 401 847 1811 **Fax:** 1 401 848 5850

e-mail: innkeeper@legendaryinnsofnewport.com

The Francis Malbone House

392 Thames Street, Newport, Rhode Island 02840

Tel: 1 401 846 0392 **Fax:** 1 401 848 5956

e-mail: innkeeper@malbone.com

THE INN AT SHADOW LAWN

120 Miantonomi Avenue, Newport, Rhode Island 02842

Tel: 1 401 847 0902 **Fax:** 1 401 848 6529

HISTORIC JACOB HILL INN

PO Box 41326, Providence, Rhode Island 02940

Tel: 1 508 336 9165 **Fax:** 1 508 336 0951

FOX CREEK INN

49 Dam Road, Chittenden, Vermont 05737

Tel: 1 802 483 6213 **Fax:** 1 802 483 2623

e-mail: foxcreek @sover.net

MOUNTAIN TOP INN & RESORT

195 Mountain Top Road, Chittenden, Vermont 05737

Tel: 1 802 483 2311 **Fax:** 1 802 483 6373

e-mail: info@mountaintopinn.com

RABBIT HILL INN

48 Lower Waterford Road, Lower Waterford, Vermont 05848

Tel: 1 802 748 5168 **Fax:** 1 802 748 8342

e-mail: info@rabbithillinn.com

1811 HOUSE

PO Box 39, Route 7A, Manchester Village, Vermont 05254

Tel: 1 802 362 1811 **Fax:** 1 802 362 2443

e-mail: house1811@adelphia.net

The Village Country Inn

Route 7A, po box 408, Manchester Village, Vermont 05254

Tel: 1 802 362 1792 **Fax:** 1 802 362 7238

Four Columns Inn

PO Box 278, Newfane, Vermont 05345

Tel: 1 802 365 7713

e-mail: innkeeper@fourcolumnsinn.com

The Mountain Road Resort At Stowe

PO Box 8, 1007 Mountain Road, Stowe, Vermont 05672

Tel: 1 802 253 4566 **Fax:** 1 802 253 7397

e-mail: stowevt@aol.com

Windham Hill Inn

West Townshend, Vermont 05359

Tel: 1 802 874 4080 **Fax:** 1 802 874 4702

The Inn At Weston

Scenic Route 100, Weston, Vermont 05161

Tel: 1 802 824 6789 **Fax:** 1 802 824 3073

e-mail: inweston@sover.net

The Jackson House Inn

114-3 Senior Lane, Woodstock, Vermont 05091

Tel: 1 802 457 2065 **Fax:** 1 802 457 9290

e-mail: innkeeper@jacksonhouse.com

WOODSTOCK INN & RESORT

Fourteen The Green, Woodstock, Vermont, 05091-1298

Tel: 1 802 457 1100 **Fax:** 1 802 457 6699

HOTEL ST FRANCIS

210 Don Gaspar Avenue, Santa Fe, New Mexico 87501

Tel: 1 505 983 5700 **Fax:** 1 505 992 6340

e-mail: david.stone@hotelstfrancis.net

BISHOP'S LODGE

PO Box 2367, Santa Fe, New Mexico, 87504

Tel: 1 505 983 6377 **Fax:** 1 505 989 8739

CASITAS AT EL MONTE

125 La Posta Road, PO Box 20, Taos, New Mexico 87671

Tel: 1 800 828 8267 **Fax:** 1 505 758 5089

THE INN ON LA LOMA PLAZA

315 Ranchitos Road, Taos, New Mexico 87571

Tel: 1 505 758 1717 **Fax:** 1 505 751 0155

e-mail: laloma@vacationtaos.com

THE BREWSTER INN

6 Ledyard Avenue, Cazenovia, New York 13035

Tel: 1 315 655 9232 **Fax:** 1 315 655 2130

ROYCROFT INN

40 South Grove Street, East Aurora, New York 14052

Tel: 1 877 652 5552 **Fax:** 1 716 655 5345

e-mail: info@roycroftinn.com

GENEVA ON THE LAKE

1001 Lochland Road (Route 14 South), Geneva, New York 14456

Tel: 1 315 789 7190 **Fax:** 1 315 789 0322

e-mail: info@GenevaOnTheLake.com

WILLIAM HENRY MILLER INN

303 North Aurora Street, Ithaca, New York 14850

Tel: 1 607 256 4553 **Fax:** 607 256 0092

e-mail: millerinn@aol.com

BRYANT PARK HOTEL

40 West 40th Street, New York, New York 10018

Tel: 1 212 869 0100 **Fax:** 1 212 869 4446

e-mail: jpalmer@phgmc.com

THE KITANO NEW YORK

66 Park Avenue New York, New York 10016

Tel: 1 212 885 7000 **Fax:** 1 212 885 7100

e-mail: reservations@kitano.com

ALBERGO ALLEGRIA

#43 Route 296, Windham, New York 12496

Tel: 1 518 734 5560 **Fax:** 1 518 734 5570

e-mail: mail@AlbergoUSA.com

SARATOGA ARMS

495–497 Broadway, Saratoga Springs, New York 12866

Tel: 1 518 584 1775 **Fax:** 1 518 581 4064

e-mail: hotel@saratoga-lodging.com

THE WRIGHT INN & CARRIAGE HOUSE

235 Pearson Drive, Asheville, North Carolina 28801

Tel: 1 828 251 0789 **Fax:** 1 828 251 0929

THEODOSIA'S BED & BREAKFAST

PO Box 3130, 2 Keelson Row, Bald Head Island, North Carolina 28461

Tel: 1 910 457 6563 **Fax:** 1 910 457 6055

e-mail: stay@theodosias.com

BALSAM MOUNTAIN INN

PO BOX 40, Balsam, North Carolina 28707

Tel: 1 828 456 9498 **Fax:** 1 828 456 9298

e-mail: balsaminn@earthlink.net

THE CEDARS INN

305 Front Street, Beaufort, North Carolina 28516

Tel: 1 252 728 7036 **Fax:** 1 252 728 1685

CHETOLA RESORT

PO Box 17, North Main Street, Blowing Rock, North Carolina 28605

Tel: 1 828 295 5500 **Fax:** 1 828 295 5529

e-mail: info@chetola.com

GIDEON RIDGE INN

PO Box 1929, Blowing Rock, North Carolina 28605

Tel: 1 828 295 3644 **Fax:** 1 828 295 4586

MILLSTONE INN

119 Lodge Lane, Hwy 64 West, Cashiers, North Carolina 28717

Tel: 1 828 743 2737 **Fax:** 1 828 743 0208

e-mail: office@millstoneinn.com

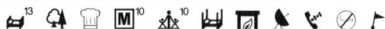

BALLANTYNE RESORT

10000 Ballantyne Commons Parkway, Charlotte, North Carolina 28277

Tel: 1 704 248 4000 **Fax:** 1 704 248 4005

e-mail: spa@ballantyneresort.com

THE PARK

2200 Rexford Road, Charlotte, North Carolina 28211

Tel: 1 704 364 8220 **Fax:** 1 704 365 4712

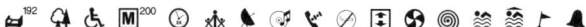

MOREHEAD MANOR BED & BREAKFAST

914 Vickers Avenue, Durham, North Carolina 27701

Tel: 1 919 687 4366 **Fax:** 1 919 687 4245

e-mail: moreheadmanorbnb@aol.com

THE LORDS PROPRIETORS' INN

300 North Broad Street, Edenton, North Carolina 27932

Tel: 1 252 482 3641 **Fax:** 1 252 482 2432

e-mail: stay@edentoninn.com

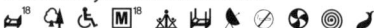

Innisfree Victorian Inn and Garden House

PO Box 469, Glenville, North Carolina 28736

Tel: 1 828 743 2946

Claddagh Inn

755 North Main Street, Hendersonville, North Carolina, 28792

Tel: 1 828 697 7778

e-mail: innkeepers@claddaghinn.com

Inn at Half Mile Farm

PO Box 2769, 214 Half Mile Drive, Highlands, North Carolina 28741

Tel: 1 828 526 8170 **Fax:** 1 828 526 2625

e-mail: halfmilefarm@aol.com

The White Doe Inn & Whispering Bay

PO Box 1029, 319 Sir Walter Raleigh Street, Manteo, North Carolina 27954

Tel: 1 252 473 9851 **Fax:** 1 252 473 4708

e-mail: whitedoe@whitedoeinn.com

The Siena Hotel

1505 E. Franklin Street, Chapel Hill, North Carolina 27514

Tel: 1 919 929 4000 **Fax:** 1 919 968 8527

e-mail: msherburne@sienahotel.com

Snowbird Mountain Lodge

275 Santeetlah Road, Robbinsville, North Carolina 28771

Tel: 1 828 479 3433   **Fax:** 1 828 479 3473

e-mail: innkeeper@snowbirdlodge.com

Pine Crest Inn

85 Pine Crest Lane, Tryon, North Carolina 28782

Tel: 1 828 859 9135 **Fax:** 1 828 859 9135

e-mail: info@pinecrestinn.com

The Swag Country Inn

2300 Swag Road, Waynesville, North Carolina 28785

Tel: 1 828 926 0430 **Fax:** 1 828 926 2036

e-mail: letters@theswag.com

The Verandas

202 NUN STREET, WILMINGTON, NORTH CAROLINA 28401-5020

Tel: 1 910 251 2212 **Fax:** 1 910 251 8932

e-mail: verandas4@aol.com

Augustus T. Zevely Inn

803 South Main Street, Winston-Salem, North Carolina 27101

Tel: 1 336 748 9299 **Fax:** 1 336 721 2211

Weasku Inn

5560 Rogue River Highway, Grants Pass, Oregon 97527

Tel: 1 541 471 8000 **Fax:** 1 541 471 7038

e-mail: info@weasku.com

Rittenhouse Square European Boutique Hotel

1715 Rittenhouse Square, Philadelphia, Pennsylvania 19103

Tel: 1 215 546 6500 **Fax:** 1 215 546 8787

e-mail: innkeeper@rittenhousebb.com

THE THOMAS BOND HOUSE

129 South 2nd Street, Philadelphia, Pennsylvania 19106

Tel: 1 215 923 8523 **Fax:** 1 215 923 8504

ROSEMARY & LOOKAWAY INN

804 Carolina Avenue, North Augusta, South Carolina 29841

Tel: 1 803 278 6222 **Fax:** 1 803 278 4877

VENDUE INN

19 Vendue Range, Charleston, South Carolina 29401

Tel: 1 843 577 7970 **Fax:** 1 843 577 2913

e-mail: vendueinnresv@aol.com

LITCHFIELD PLANTATION

Kings River Road, Box 290, Pawleys Island, South Carolina 29585

Tel: 1 843 237 9121 **Fax:** 1 843 237 1041

e-mail: vacation@litchfieldplantation.com

LA BASTIDE

10 Road Of Vines, Travelers Rest, South Carolina 29690

Tel: 1 864 836 8463 **Fax:** 1 864 836 4820

e-mail: labastide@mindspring.com

WHITESTONE COUNTRY INN

1200 Paint Rock Road, Kingston, Tennessee 37763

Tel: 1 865 376 0113 **Fax:** 1 865 376 4454

e-mail: moreinfo@whitestoneinn.com

Blackberry Farm

1471 West Millers Cove Road, Walland, Great Smoky Mountains, Tennessee 37886

Tel: 1 865 380 2260 **Fax:** 1 865 681 7753

e-mail: info@blackberryfarm.com

Ye Kendall Inn

128 West Blanco, Boerne, Texas 78006

Tel: 1 830 249 2138 **Fax:** 1 830 249 7371

e-mail: info@yekendallinn.com

The Adolphus

1321 Commerce Street, Dallas, Texas 75202

Tel: 1 214 742 8200 **Fax:** 1 214 651 3563

The Inn Above Onion Creek

4444 Highway 150 West, Kyle, Texas 78640

Tel: 1 888 579 7686 **Fax:** 1 512 268 1090

e-mail: info@innaboveonioncreek.com

Havana River Walk Inn

1015 Navarro, San Antonio, Texas 78205

Tel: 1 210 222 2008 **Fax:** 1 210 222 2717

e-mail: info@havanariverwalkinn.com

Kiepersol Estates

21508 Merlot Lane, Tyler, Texas 75703

Tel: 1 903 894 3300 **Fax:** 1 903 894 4140

e-mail: bandb@kiepersol.com

200 South Street Inn

200 South Street, Charlottesville, Virginia, 22902

Tel: 1 434 979 0200 **Fax:** 1 434 979 4403

e-mail: southst@cstone.net

Clifton - The Country Inn & Estate

1296 Clifton Inn Drive, Charlottesville, Virginia 22911

Tel: 1 434 971 1800 **Fax:** 1 434 971 7098

Prospect Hill Plantation Inn

PO Box 6909, Charlottesville, VIRGINIA 22906

Tel: 1 540 967 0844 **Fax:** 1 540 967 0102

Prince Michel Restaurant & Suites

Prince Michel de Virginia, HCR 4, Box 77, Leon, Virginia 22725

Tel: 1 540 547 9720 **Fax:** 1 540 547 3088

e-mail: info@princemichel.com

The Goodstone Inn & Estate

36205 Snake Hill Road, Middleburg, Virginia 20117

Tel: 1 540 687 4645 **Fax:** 1 540 687 6115

e-mail: information@goodstone.com

Willow Grove Inn

14079 Plantation Way, Orange, Virginia 22960

Tel: 1 540 672 5982 **Fax:** 1 540 672 3674

FREDERICK HOUSE

28 North New Street, Staunton, Virginia 24401

Tel: 1 540 885 4220 **Fax:** 1 540 885 5180

e-mail: stay@frederickhouse.com

L'AUBERGE PROVENÇALE

PO Box 190, White Post, Virginia 22663

Tel: 1 540 837 1375 **Fax:** 1 540 837 2004

LEGACY OF WILLIAMSBURG INN

930 James Towmn Road, Williamsburg, Virginia 23185–3917

Tel: 1 757 220 0524 **Fax:** 1 757 220 2211

e-mail: legacy@tni.net

NAGLE WARREN MANSION

222 East 17Th Street, Cheyenne, Wyoming 82001

Tel: 1 307 637 3333 **Fax:** 1 307 638 6879

e-mail: jostenfoss@aol.com

Mexico

CASA NATALIA

Blvd Mijares 4, San Jose Del Cabo, Baja California Sur 23400

Tel: 52 624 14 251 00 **Fax:** 52 624 14251 10

e-mail: casa.natalia@1cabonet.com.mx

Villas Tacul

Boulevard Kukulkan, KM 5.5, Cancun, Quintana Roo, 77500 Mexico

Tel: 52 998 883 00 00 **Fax:** 52 998 849 70 70

e-mail: vtacul@cancun.com.mx

La Casa De Los Sueños

Carretera Garrafon, S/N Isla Mujeres, Quintana Roo, Mexico 77400

Tel: 52 99887 70651 **Fax:** 52 99887 70708

e-mail: info@lossuenos.com

Maroma

Highway 307 km 51, Riviera Maya, Quintana Roo, 77710 Mexico

Tel: 52 998 872 8200 **Fax:** 52 998 872 8220

e-mail: reservations@maromahotel.com

Hotel Villa Del Sol

Playa La Ropa S/N, PO Box 84, Zihuatanejo 40880, Mexico

Tel: 52 755 4 2239/3239 **Fax:** 52 7554 2758/4066

e-mail: hotel@villasol.com.mx

Bermuda

Ariel Sands

34 South Shore Road, Devonshire, Bermuda

Tel: 1 441 236 1010 **Fax:** 1 441 236 0087

e-mail: reservations@arielsands.com

Rosedon Hotel

PO Box Hm 290, Hamilton Hmax, Bermuda

Tel: 1 441 295 1640 **Fax:** 1 441 295 5904

e-mail: rosedon@ibl.bm

BERMUDA - PAGET

Fourways Inn

PO Box Pg 294, Paget Pg Bx, Bermuda

Tel: 1 441 236 6517 **Fax:** 1 441 236 5528

e-mail: info@fourways.com

BERMUDA - PAGET

Newstead Hotel

27 Harbour Road, Paget Pg02, Bermuda

Tel: 1 441 236 6060 **Fax:** 1 441 236 7454

e-mail: reservations@newsteadhotel.com

BERMUDA - SOMERSET

Cambridge Beaches

Kings Point, Somerset, MA02 Bermuda

Tel: 1 441 234 0331 **Fax:** 1 441 234 3352

e-mail: cambeach@ibl.bm

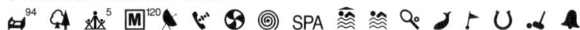

BERMUDA - SOUTHAMPTON

The Reefs

56 South Shore Road, Southampton, SN02 Bermuda

Tel: 1 441 238 0222 **Fax:** 1 441 238 8372

e-mail: reefsbda@ibl.bm

BERMUDA - WARWICK

Surf Side Beach Club

90 South Shore Road, Warwick, Bermuda

Tel: 1 441 236 7100 **Fax:** 1 441 236 9765

e-mail: surf@ibl.bm

The Caribbean

Frangipani Beach Club

PO Box 1378, Meads Bay, Anguilla, West Indies
Tel: 1 264 497 6442/6444 **Fax:** 1 264 497 6440
e-mail: frangipani@anguillanet.com

Blue Waters

PO BOX 256, ST JOHNS, ANTIGUA, WEST INDIES
Tel: 1 268 462 0290 **Fax:** 1 268 462 0293
e-mail: res@bluewaters.net

Curtain Bluff

PO Box 288, Antigua, West Indies
Tel: 1 268 462 8400 **Fax:** 1 268 462 8409

Galley Bay

Five Islands, PO Box 305, St John's, Antigua, West Indies
Tel: 1 268 462 0302 **Fax:** 1 268 462 4551

The Inn at English Harbour

Po Box 187, St Johns, Antigua, West Indies
Tel: 1 268 460 1014 **Fax:** 1 268 460 1603
e-mail: theinn@candw.ag

Coral Reef Club

St. James, Barbados, West Indies

Tel: 1 246 422 2372 **Fax:** 1 246 422 1776

e-mail: coral@caribsurf.com

The Sandpiper

Holetown, St. James, Barbados, West Indies

Tel: 1 246 422 2251 **Fax:** 1 246 422 0900

e-mail: coral@caribsurf.com

Avila Beach Hotel

Penstraat 130, Willemstad, Curaçao, Netherlands Antilles, West Indies

Tel: 599 9 461 4377 **Fax:** 599 9 461 1493

e-mail: info@avilahotel.com

Spice Island Beach Resort

Grand Anse Beach, Box 6, St. George's, Grenada, West Indies

Tel: 1 473 444 4423 **Fax:** 1 473 444 4807

e-mail: spiceisl@caribsurf.com

Blue Lagoon Villas

Fairy Hill, Port Antonio, Jamaica, West Indies

Tel: 1 876 993 7701 **Fax:** 1 876 993 8492

e-mail: reservations@bluelagoonvillas.com

Grand Lido Sans Souci

PO Box 103, Ocho Rios, St Ann, Jamaica, West Indies

Tel: 1 876 994 1206 **Fax:** 1 876 994 1544

Half Moon Golf, Tennis & Beach Club

Montego Bay, Jamaica, West Indies

Tel: 1 876 953 2211 **Fax:** 1 876 953 2731

e-mail: reservations@halfmoonclub.com

Mocking Bird Hill

PO Box 254, Port Antonio, Jamaica

Tel: 1 876 993 7134 **Fax:** 1 876 993 7133

e-mail: mockbrd@cwjamaica.com

The Hermitage

Nevis, West Indies

Tel: 1 869 469 3477 **Fax:** 1 869 469 2481

e-mail: nevherm@caribsurf.com

Montpelier Plantation Inn

Montpelier Estate, PO Box 474, Nevis, West Indies

Tel: 1 869 469 3462 **Fax:** 1 869 469 2932

e-mail: info@montpeliernevis.com

Nisbet Plantation Beach Club

St James Parish, Nevis, West Indies

Tel: +1 869 469 9325 **Fax:** +1 869 469 9864

e-mail: nisbetbc@caribsurf.com

The Golden Lemon

Dieppe Bay, St Kitts, West Indies

Tel: 1 869 465 7260 **Fax:** 1 869 465 4019

e-mail: info@goldenlemon.com

Ottley's Plantation Inn

Po Box 345, Basseterre, St Kitts, West Indies

Tel: 1 869 465 7234 **Fax:** 1 869 465 4760

e-mail: ottleys@caribsurf.com

Rawlins Plantation Inn

PO Box 340, St Kitts, West Indies

Tel: 1 869 465 6221 **Fax:** 1 869 465 4954

e-mail: rawplant@caribsurf.com

Anse Chastanet

PO Box 7000, Soufriere, St. Lucia, West Indies

Tel: 1 758 459 7000 **Fax:** 1 758 459 7700

e-mail: ansechastanet@candw.lc

Mago Estate Hotel

PO Box 247, Soufrière, St Lucia, West Indies

Tel: 1 758 459 5880 **Fax:** 1 758 459 7352

e-mail: info@magohotel.com

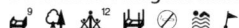

Camelot Inn - A Boutique Hotel

PO Box 787, Kingstown, The Grenadines, St Vincent, West Indies

Tel: 1 784 456 2100 **Fax:** 1 784 456 2233

e-mail: caminn@caribsurf.com

Grand View Beach Hotel

Villa Point, Box 173, St Vincent, West Indies

Tel: 1 784 458 4811 **Fax:** 1 784 457 4174

e-mail: grandview@caribsurf.com

Palm Island

St Vincent & The Grenadines, West Indies
Tel: 1 800 345 0271 **Fax:** 1 954 481 1661
e-mail: res@classicislands.com

Point Grace

PO Box 700, Providenciales, Turks and Caicos Islands, British west indies
Tel: 1 649 946 5096 **Fax:** 1 649 946 5097
e-mail: reservations@pointgrace.com

SPA

The Sands at Grace Bay

PO BOX 681, PROVIDENCIALES, TURKS & CAICOS islands, british WEST INDIES
Tel: 1 649 946 5199 **Fax:** 1 649 946 5198
e-mail: vacations@thesandsresort.com

Pacific

Nukubati Island

PO Box 1928, Labasa, Fiji Islands
Tel: 61 2 93888 196 **Fax:** 61 2 93888 204
e-mail: nukubatihq@msn.com.au

Blue Lagoon Cruises

183 Vitogo Parade, Lautoka, Fiji Islands
Tel: 1 679 6661 622 **Fax:** 1 679 6664 098
e-mail: blc@is.com.fj

NAMALE

Savu Savu, Fiji Islands

Tel: 1 858 535 6380 **Fax:** 1 858 535 6385

e-mail: namalefiji@aol.com

THE WAKAYA CLUB

Wakaya island, Fiji Islands

Tel: 1 970 927 2044 **Fax:** 1 970 927 2048

e-mail: info@wakaya.com

TOBERUA ISLAND RESORT

PO Box 3332, Nausori, Fiji Islands

Tel: 679 347 2777 **Fax:** 679 347 2888

e-mail: toberua@connect.com.fj

VOMO ISLAND

Po Box 5650, Lautoka, Fiji Islands

Tel: 679 6668 122 **Fax:** 679 6668 500

e-mail: sales@vomo.com.fj

TURTLE ISLAND

Yasawa Islands, Po Box 9317, Nadi Airport, Nadi, Fiji Islands

Tel: 61 3 9823 8300 **Fax:** 61 3 9823 8383

e-mail: info@turtlefiji.com.au

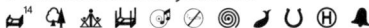

YASAWA ISLAND RESORT

PO Box 10128, Nadi Airport, Nadi, Fiji Islands

Tel: 679 772 2266 **Fax:** 679 772 4456

e-mail: yasawa@is.com.fj

AGGIE GREY'S HOTEL

PO Box 67, Apia, Samoa

Tel: 685 228 80 **Fax:** 685 236 26 or 685 23203

e-mail: aggiegreys@aggiegreys.com

CONDÉ NAST JOHANSENS GUIDES

All the recommendations in this Pocket Guide can be found in our range of published guides. The guides contain further information about each property including large colour pictures, descriptive text, directions, price details and location maps.

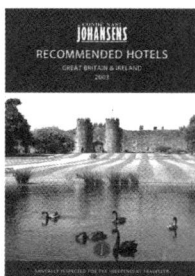

RECOMMENDED HOTELS, GREAT BRITAIN & IRELAND

440 unique and luxurious hotels, town houses, castles and manor houses chosen for their superior standards and individual character

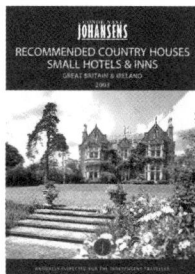

RECOMMENDED COUNTRY HOUSES, SMALL HOTELS & INNS, GREAT BRITAIN & IRELAND

282 smaller more rural properties, ideal for short breaks or more intimate stays

CONDÉ NAST JOHANSENS GUIDES

To order these guides please call
From the UK: FREEPHONE 0800 269 397
From Europe: +44 208 655 7810
From the US: TOLL FREE 1-800-564-7518

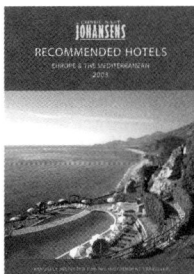

RECOMMENDED HOTELS, EUROPE & THE MEDITERRANEAN

324 continental gems featuring châteaux, resorts and charming countryside hotels

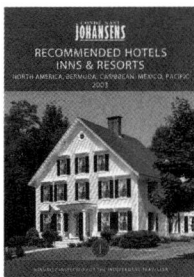

RECOMMENDED HOTELS, INNS & RESORTS, NORTH AMERICA, BERMUDA, CARIBBEAN, MEXICO, PACIFIC

199 properties including many hidden delights from across the region

WWW.JOHANSENS.COM

Visit the Condé Nast Johansens web site to:

- Print out detailed **road maps**

- See up to date accommodation **Special Offers**

- Access each **recommended hotel's own website**

- Find details of places to visit nearby -
  **historic houses, castles, gardens, museums
  and galleries**

Condé Nast Johansens Home Page

*Search for
hotels and
business venues*

*Access local
places to visit*

*Link to latest
Special Offers*

*Users can log in as an Online Member to receive regular e-mail
updates, complete guest survey reports and create their own
Personal Portfolio of favourite recommended hotels*

Example of Recommended Hotel's Web Entry

*Access the
hotel's contact
details, website
and e-mail*

*See the latest
Special Offers
for this hotel*

*Link to a
detailed local
area map*